Swimming with Dolphins in New Zealand

By the same author

The Elingamite and Its Treasure
Beneath New Zealand Seas
Sharks and Other Ancestors
Islands of Survival
Fishes of the New Zealand Region
The Cliff Dwellers
Diving for Treasure
Dolphin Dolphin
The Burning of the Boyd
Ocean Planet
Encounters with Whales & Dolphins
Wade Doak's World of New Zealand Fishes
The New Zealand Diver's Guide

Swimming with Dolphins in New Zealand

WADE DOAK

Hodder & Stoughton
A member of the Hodder Headline Group

For humans of the future, in the fervent hope that you too may share, with the people whose stories appear here, that moment of ecstasy when we meet with dolphins in the wild.

© 1994 Wade Doak
First published in New Zealand by Hodder Headline NZ Ltd, 1994

ISBN 0–340–57571–9

All rights reserved. No part of this publication may be reproduced or transmitted in any form or by any means, electronic or mechanical, including photocopying, recording, or any information storage and retrieval system, without permission in writing from the publisher.

Design and production by Pressgang, 17 Sale Street, Auckland 1.
Illustrations and maps by Sandra Parkkali.
Made and printed in Singapore for Hodder & Stoughton, a division of Hodder Headline PLC, 44–46 View Road, Glenfield, Auckland, New Zealand.

Contents

Foreword: Wade Doak & the Dolphins, by Hugo Verlomme   7
Preface: Playing with Dolphins   11
Acknowledgements   13
Prologue: Quest for Ocean Mind   15

Part One: Pathways to Dolphin Encounter

1. Project Interlock Begins   19
2. Dolphin Body Language   23
3. The Sound Channel   26
4. Interlocks with Common Dolphins   28
5. Interval: A New Approach   41
6. Interlocks with Bottlenose Dolphins   48
7. Simo & the Keeper's Wife   58

Part Two: New Zealand Dolphin Swimming Locations

8. Project Interlock Extends   65
9. Far North Dolphin Encounters   70
10. Dolphin Encounters in the Poor Knights Area   81
11. Dolphin Swimming in the Hauraki Gulf   96
12. Swimming with Bay of Plenty Dolphins   110
13. Dolphin Swimming at Kapiti Island   121
14. Dolphins & Swimmers in Cook Strait   127
15. Dolphin swimming in the Marlborough Sounds   133
16. Swimming with Dolphins at Kaikoura   138
17. Swimming with Dolphins in the Deep South   141

Part Three: The Modern Era

18. Commercial Dolphin Swimming Operations   147

Conclusion: Project Interlock International   155

Epilogue: On Play   158

Foreword: Wade Doak & the Dolphins

BY HUGO VERLOMME

By turn diving pioneer, underwater hunter, undersea film-maker, treasure diver, researcher into reef fish and shark behaviour, oceanographer and anthropologist, Wade Doak has devoted his life to the ocean. But since 1975 dolphins have been his main preoccupation . . .

Convinced that saltwater is good for the newborn, Lorna Doak was bathing her baby in the sea one day in April 1940, at New Brighton beach, New Zealand. Suddenly a rogue wave tore the child from her hands. As the receding waters carried him away, she must have thought her little boy was lost forever in the waters of the Pacific. As luck would have it, another wave brought him back, safe and sound.

Has this anything to do with her naming him Wade? It is the name of a giant in Norse legend who walked across the fiords to carry off young virgins and devour them. But in English 'to wade' means to 'walk in the water'. From the start Wade Doak's destiny seemed to be connected with the ocean.

The stories of his obsession with the ocean are dizzying. He grew up at some distance from the sea but haunted the local swimming pools. He soon found he preferred to swim in the calm depths of a pool rather than on the surface among a maelstrom of kids. With some friends he practised gathering coins on the bottom and increasing his breath-holding capacity.

Then, at 12, he discovered the magic portal to the underwater realm: a diving mask. For Wade and his cobbers, such a discovery extended their dives to incredible durations: one, on the edge of blackout, stayed below for almost five minutes.

Inspired by Greek legends and the novels of Jules Verne and Victor Hugo, at 15 Wade decided to build a diving helmet from an old ice-cream can. On a Lyttelton Harbour wharf his friends pumped air down to him with a car tyre pump. He explored the murky depths of the harbour 6 metres down, on a mission worthy of Captain Nemo.

Before long, on one of those harbour dives, he stumbled on an old relic in the mud—some sort of metal vase covered in weed. Surfacing, he left it perched on a rock at low tide. Next day he was astounded to read in the paper that a line fisherman had snagged an archaeological treasure of great value—a chalice, no doubt lost by a colonist in the previous century . . . Perhaps it was to pay back fate that Wade became, some years later, a treasure hunter.

Devoted and resourceful, his inventiveness brings to mind a French diving pioneer: commander Yves Le Prieur, who truly was the inventor of the self-contained underwater breathing apparatus (scuba) in 1925, testing it at the Trocadero aquarium in 1934.

At 15 years of age Wade Doak discovered undersea freedom using scuba tanks. From that time a complete new universe opened up before him. And from then on nothing could deter him from this all-embracing summons, distracting him more and more from his school studies in the humanities.

In his biography *Ocean Planet* we find him in a diving suit on the bank of the Avon River, Christchurch, reading Shakespeare while waiting for a crane to install the next sections of sewer pipe which he had to bolt together to earn money. Always ready to dive, Wade even got the job of laying concrete underwater for reservoirs at the new Canterbury University at Ilam.

At this time, on the other side of the world, another group of diving pioneers was discovering undersea marvels. Cousteau, Dumas, Diolé, Tailliez, the 'sea-musketeers' and their followers, were exploring the blue depths of the Mediterranean, taking photos and making films to immortalise their exploits.

On this planet, somebody is always awake. In 1958, when the French divers were going to bed, on the other side of the world, Wade Doak and his friends Kelly Tarlton, Keith Gordon and Jaan Voot were setting out, just like them, to hunt fish, to take photos, and to make films beneath the sea.

But this thirst for the ocean was not all. In June 1959 with Keith he launched a little magazine, *Dive*, devoted to the development of diving. Seven years later it became an internationally recognised bimonthly.

In 1960 Wade met a young woman who was keen to improve her diving ability. It was Jan. They set off for New Caledonia on an undersea honeymoon. Even in her eighth month of pregnancy, Jan continued to dive. Not surprisingly their son Brady was capable of accompanying his parents to 30 metres at the age of 11. Nowadays he makes underwater filming expeditions to many parts of the Pacific and the Antarctic. Their daughter Karla started scuba-diving with her mother at nine.

Pursuing their passion Wade and Jan decided to live at one of the finest places for diving in New Zealand: the Poor Knights area in the far north. But it isn't always easy to earn a living when addicted to diving.

Then, one day in 1966, during an expedition for his magazine *Dive*, Wade and a team of divers found a shipwreck. And not just any wreck. It was the *Elingamite*, famous in New Zealand as a tragic turn–of-the-century shipping loss with a fortune in gold and silver aboard. And so, for Wade, Kelly Tarlton, Jaan Voot and other companions, a new vocation: they became treasure salvagers.

Their expeditions were crowned with success. After multiple attempts they managed to raise 50,000 coins. Their story went around the world. Wade wrote his first book and with Kelly Tarlton worked on his first film to relate this undersea adventure. Could the dream become reality: earning a living exploring further shipwrecks, publishing a diving magazine, selling underwater photos, and writing books about the sea?

Little by little Wade discovered that the real treasure is the living ocean. Fascinated, he began exploring the unique undersea cliffs, caves and reefs of the Poor Knights Islands. And it was alone there, in one of the most immense marine caves in the world, that he met his first dolphins—a meeting in 1971 that had the power of an initiation rite in the vast Rikoriko Cave, to the early Maori a sacred place. In their language 'rikoriko' means both the echoing of sound and the sparkling of light. It was a magical place for Wade Doak, who would never be the same after this encounter. A seed had been planted in his mind.

At this time he was preoccupied with the behaviour of reef fish. His dream: to be able to dive among them and recognise each species by name and understand their social lives. He induced diving biologists to come on undersea rambles at the Poor Knights. With their knowledge he was able to bring out three books on the undersea life of New Zealand and on the social lives of fishes.

A short time later Australian biologist Barry Russell invited him to join an expedition in the South Pacific financed by the National Geographic Society. Wild with joy he went to sea aboard the little oceanographic research ship *El Torito* captained by none other than Dr Walter Stark, a famous American ocean scientist and inventor—a man who had, in Wade's eyes, as much prestige as Cousteau himself.

This was to be the first of a series of South Sea Islands expeditions. Walter Stark, deeply interested in sharks, tested on himself the zebra suit (with the pattern of a venomous sea snake) to see whether it would repel sharks. Isn't imitation the first step towards communication? Without doubt inspired by these experiments, Wade was later to create his dolphin suit.

With Walter Stark and *El Torito*, Wade studied shark behaviour and, then, the lives of a Melanesian people who have a shark-worshipping religion.

The ocean explorations of Walter Stark are related by Wade Doak in his two books *Sharks and Other Ancestors* and *Islands of Survival*.

Wade Doak was resuming his own ocean studies when one April day in 1975, after a superb day's diving at the Poor Knights with a group of biologist friends, he had his second encounter with dolphins. The seed planted earlier in his mind by the Rikoriko Cave encounter was copiously watered. From that time forward his entire life hinged on the world of dolphins. It almost seemed as if the ultimate goal of his existence had been shaped by the ocean towards a sudden moment of communication with these sea creatures, a little like an extra-terrestrial species.

Contrary to traditional researchers, Wade Doak did not seek to study dolphins in captivity. On the contrary, he set out to meet them in their own element and on their terms. Few people today have spent more time with these creatures in the wild.

Garnering the knowledge of other divers and sharing it around, Wade and Jan Doak established Project Interlock, a global network which has brought together over many years all sorts of encounters between humans and cetaceans.

After listening to the dolphins for years, he offers us his intuitions, his understandings and his deepest doubts. You will find some fine lines. Revelations will unfold . . .

Reading Wade Doak, one is obliged to admit that the dolphin is very different from other mammals, just as, on land, the human is. Human/dolphin—it is strange that these words have a certain resemblance. In Greek *delphis* is the womb from which life emerges. One thing distinguishes the dolphin from other animals—its attitude towards humans—a perfect example of philanthropy. Although we massacre them every day and hold them in prison, wild dolphins never turn on us. Why? What are their capacities? The enigma of the dolphin raises more and more questions and passionate imaginings. Wade Doak's writings show that it is the truth that is so much more surprising.

(Translated from *Wade Doak: Ambassadeur des Dauphins,* by Hugo Verlomme, J.C. Lattès, Paris, 1993.)

Preface: Playing with Dolphins

Essentially this book is about humans who have rediscovered how to play. Fascination with the kinetic poetry of dolphins compels us to make huge efforts to engage their interest—or we are quickly left staring into the blue. To satisfy our lust for their beauteous forms, humans have tried capturing dolphins and imprisoning them in jails, but inevitably their magic, like cut flowers, is lost. Perhaps this is the ultimate paradox for humans, whose every whim technology seeks to satisfy: we can only truly encounter other life forms on their own terms, in the wild. And for the dolphins, the terms for spending time with us are: playfulness.

Dolphin swimming is a dream shared by humans all the world over—even those who have never seen the sea. Perhaps some intuitive wisdom is driving us towards the rediscovery of play, which, scientists have found, persists into adulthood according to brain capacity . . .

Could 'play loss' be the missing element in human societies all the world over that makes us the 'naked killer ape'? Is it the key to our aggression? When big-brain mammals are bored, they are dangerous.

When I was a boy, stories of humans climbing into the sky were favourites of the young. Mount Everest was a continuation of Jack and the Bean Stalk, but climber after climber died on its slopes. Then, one day in 1953, I recall seeing a newspaper billboard in Christchurch announcing that Tenzing and Hillary had reached the summit. Nowadays people walk up there in tour parties; people climb it alone, without oxygen. Yet the mountain has not changed. Just knowing it can be done is the only major difference.

I have a friend whose nose was broken by a jealous solitary dolphin. Possessiveness is a trait we share with dolphins, regardless of how angelic some folk may fantasise them to be. For me it is a tragic mistake to deify dolphins—or even to regard them as humans with fins. In so doing we miss the most precious point: they possess many of our uglier traits, but appear to have climbed that Mount Everest of interpersonal relationships. They have the lethal capacity to terminate another, or a human life, by ramming with their beaks. *But they never do it.* If one species has climbed that Mount Everest, maybe there is hope for us. And if we learn all we can from encounters with dolphins, maybe we'll come a little closer to that universal nonlethal relationship with each other. One thing is clear: they have been around a lot longer than *Homo sapiens*. It gives us hope.

But why do they extend their golden rule to our species when humans do them so much harm? A few months ago New Zealand's solo dolphin Maui at Kaikoura gave Anna Levin, a special friend of hers (and ours), a salmon—a rare delicacy, as these fishes are not native to our waters. But there is a salmon farm to the north from which it may have escaped. Aihe, our other solo dolphin in Golden Bay, gave a young girl a blue fin tuna, much too big for a dolphin to swallow. But neither of these solo dolphins would accept fish from humans. They just seek social stimulation and especially enjoy a sensitive, long-term relationship with somebody who will brave the cold of winter to play with them.

These gifts of fish that dolphins all over the world have offered humans make me wonder if there could be an ancient symbiotic relationship in which humans have almost forgotten their half of the bargain. I have studied many symbiotic relationships in the sea and found it quite miraculous that fishes *never* harm their symbiont cleaner fishes or cleaner shrimps. This means that consistent, universal forbearance can function at a rather basic level: 'wired in'.

The urge most humans have to swim with dolphins should not be ignored: it could well be a primal and benevolent drive too long suppressed to our detriment, leaving us bereft and cut off from nature. It is, as dolphin swimmers have put it, nature's ultimate adventure.

Part One of this book explains how, back in the seventies, Jan Doak and I became intrigued with the possibility of learning about dolphins by engaging their interest through body language and sound channels. Having learnt how to gain their trust and explore creative play with them, we set up Project Interlock, publishing our experiences widely and feeding back those of others to the public in order to gain further insights.

Part Two presents the results of this research. A tour of dolphin swim locations in New Zealand, it provides the reader with insights into how to play with dolphins. Accounts range from brief encounters to complex, prolonged affairs that indicate the dolphins were deeply engaged in exploring the water people.

Some would-be dolphin swimmers might like me to write a step-by-step 'how to' manual, but such an approach would be futile. By its very nature, interlock with another species requires spontaneity and improvisation. At least by reading of the successes and failures presented here, more resources may come to mind and you may be less likely to simply stare at those bionic torpedoes—or to grab at them.

Part Three brings us to the modern era, where something quite extraordinary has developed in New Zealand: uniquely, all around our coast, four species of dolphin have begun to accept the regular approaches of dolphin swim tour operators who are taking out people from all over the world with dreams of meeting dolphins in the wild.

On a planet where six billion humans threaten to double their population in the next 40 years, within the lifetimes of our newborn, these interlocks have a special importance. Unless a significant number of humans can have inspirational experiences of nature, such as those provided by these unique sea creatures, ambassadors for the global environment, we risk overwhelming the planet with our pollution and ruthless competition for the ocean's dwindling resources. Global awareness of dolphins' specialness, the extraordinarily positive effect meeting them has on our species, and the respect this creates for their right to live, may tip the scales in favour of all life forms on this planet, whereon humans may find their true place as symbionts rather than harmful parasites: 'Play is an act of trust in life'.*

Acknowledgements

If I were to thank all the people who have assisted Project Interlock in the collection of the material presented here, this book would resemble a telephone directory. So many people mentioned here have become valued friends to both Jan and me and to the dolphins we all love so dearly. We often say to each other that it is the people we contact during our research into dolphins, as much as the dolphins themselves, that make it all so worthwhile.

I would like to give special thanks to the Department of Conservation staff who have helped us, especially Mike Donoghue and Andrew Baxter.

Our dear friends Hal Chapman, Sheryl Gibney, Barry Fenn, Bill Clementson, Hugo Verlomme, and Jeroen Jongejans, and my son, Brady Doak, have given us so much support and encouragement over the years. And so have Bill Shanks, Ramari Stewart, Colin Lee and Des Crossland, Waipu Pita, Witi McMath, Peter Munroe, Eric Kircher, Tony and Avril Ayling, Gwen Struik and Roger Bray, Gary Tee, Malcolm Pitt, and Max Clift.

Then there are the dolphin swim operators and guides who have helped us to piece together a composite picture of a rapidly emerging miracle—the new dolphin swim industry: Jo Berghan, Steve Stembridge, Elizabeth and Rod Rae, Carol Seguin and Craig Posa, Zoe and Les Battersby, Brent McFadden, Brian Betts, Dennis Buurman, and Ivan McIntosh.

Finally, I wish to thank Project Jonah and Greenpeace for their

* *Playing by Heart* by Fred Donaldson.

consistent support over the years. We urge readers of this book who want to help dolphins and whales to support them generously.

Project Jonah: PO Box 8376, Symonds Street, Auckland. Phone (09) 302-3106.

Greenpeace NZ Inc.: Private Bag, Wellesley Street, Auckland. Phone (09) 377-6128.

Prologue: Quest for Ocean Mind

Since I wrote the prologue with that title in my previous book *Encounters with Whales & Dolphins* (1988) a major advance has occurred. Science now accepts that we humans are not alone. Other animals do have the capacity to think. Some have been proven to function at the level of human infants. The ethical implications of this discovery are not for science to resolve. Are we humans going to extend moral rights to other sentient creatures?

An important step has to be encountering large-brain creatures in the wild, in open-ended, creative situations, and learning their needs and capacities. Fortunately, with cetaceans this is now taking place and nowhere more rapidly than in New Zealand.

My previous book on cetacean encounters was global in scope. At that time I needed the whole world to draw on for experiences that illustrate each major aspect of human/cetacean encounter. But the personal experiences that launched me into this study all took place in New Zealand. It is fitting that five years later I can now provide a special edition that accomplishes those same goals yet concentrates entirely on the astonishing development of encounters in this country—to the point where New Zealand now leads the world in dolphin-swim opportunities and has few rivals in its cetacean tourism. I am told that my books have played an important role in that process. I hope these pages may further the growth of human/cetacean relationships in a country that values these creatures so highly. New Zealand is undoubtedly at the forefront of developing a new ethic towards nonhuman awareness, which, in the case of cetaceans, I like to call ocean mind.

We Are Not Alone

Did the ability to plot mischief, form plans, manipulate symbols, and express feelings exist before the earliest humanlike creatures walked the earth, some five to seven million years ago?

Science writer Eugene Linden has boldly answered this question in the affirmative:

'Since antiquity, philosophers have argued that higher mental abilities—in short, thinking and language—are the great divide separating humans from other species. The lesser creatures, René Descartes contended in 1637, are little more than automatons, sleepwalking through life without a mote of self-awareness. The French thinker found it inconceivable that an animal might have the ability to "use words or signs, putting them together as we do".

'Charles Darwin delivered an unsettling blow to this doctrine a century ago when he asserted that humans were linked by common ancestry to the rest of the animal kingdom. Darwinism raised a series of tantalising questions for future generations: If other vertebrates are similar to humans in blood and bone, should they not share other characteristics, including intelligence?'*

Linden offers an overview of research currently in progress with captive apes, parrots, sealions and dolphins that provides convincing scientific evidence that other species do share with us 'some higher mental abilities'. Reputable studies show an ape learning sign language as a human child would, in the course of daily activities; dolphins learning a gestural language and manipulating their vocabularies symbolically; sealions demonstrating some of the learning skills that are needed to use language; and a grey parrot using language to get attention and maintain social contact.

Eugene Linden concludes that other social animals besides man have evolved the capacity to understand and manipulate symbols—i.e., intelligence. For social animals there is pressure to keep track of complex relationships: 'To know whom to trust'.

Before reading of similar experiences gained from noncaptive animals, I offer you Eugene Linden's inspired words:

'The fact that nature may have broadly sown the seeds of consciousness suggests a world enlivened by many different minds.'

* *Time* cover story, 'Can Animals Think?' (29 March 1993).

Part One:
Pathways to Dolphin Encounter

'Wherever dolphins have impinged on a human mind it seems a deep and resonant chord is struck; something that is bringing our species together, perhaps closer than ever before.'

—Wade Doak

1: Project Interlock Begins

Dolphins entered my life at a most appropriate time, because a major phase of diving exploration had just been completed and I had photo files bulging with pictures of the myriad life forms found in warm southern seas—but never a dolphin.

My photo collection had begun in 1959, when a hoard of silver coins salvaged from the treasure ship *Elingamite* gave me the nest egg that led to full-time study of marine life. Until then I'd been a teacher with a language degree and a passion for the undersea world. Quitting the classroom, I devoted a dozen years to illustrating and researching books about reef fish behaviour and the ecology of invertebrate creatures on the undersea cliff. Then I wrote a further two books on the explorations of *El Torito*, the undersea research vessel belonging to American scientist Dr Walter Starck. With him, and later my whole family, I spent several sun-drenched years exploring coral reefs and their inhabitants, from polyp to atoll dweller, sharks and shark worshippers.

In fact, when I think back on it, the yarn I'd had with Walt in the saloon of *El Torito* probably triggered something that set me off in the direction of this book. We were riding out a hurricane in the lagoon at Lord Howe Island when this leading diving biologist began relating his life story for me.

Walt had some formative childhood experiences in Florida Keys, where his father was a charter-boat skipper. 'This day my father caught a baby dolphin for a dolphin pool. The mother stood by our boat making such piteous sounds that my own mother called on him to release it. This must be the only animal that has the power to kill a man, but always forbears to use it, even in a situation like that. Among dolphins themselves, there just doesn't seem to be any lethal aggression, and they accept man on the same level.'

For some reason I always remembered Walt's avowal that, if he ever had the means, he would devote himself to solving the dolphin enigma. I was, and still am, inspired by that ambition.

In all my diving life dolphins had been peripheral to the undersea world I was exploring. For most divers around at that time it was typically a hello-goodbye type of encounter. Dolphins fled if we tried to jump in with them from a boat. I'd only once had a longer acquaintance.

In May 1971, at the Poor Knights Islands, 22 kilometres off the east coast of northern New Zealand, I had been 20 metres down where white sand lies in drifts at the foot of the Rikoriko Cave wall. Suddenly everything went black. I glanced up in fear. The cave portal, usually a blaze of blue fire, had dimmed. It was seething with huge shapes—sharp fins, fast tails, and jaws. Dolphins. One of them, in silhouette on the surface, smacked its tail, and a pair of curving forms glided down in a spiral, circling me and rising. Each time the leader of this game smacked with his tail, a pair spiralled down, curving on their sides to gaze intently as they passed me. Enchanted, I forgot for some time that I had a camera. Then with the last two frames left on the film I took my first dolphin pictures —*Tursiops truncatus*, the bottlenose. A seed was sown. After our *El Torito* adventures, my family settled down to a rural life in a small cottage beside a mangrove river in Northland. It was one evening in April 1975, after a superb day's diving at the Poor Knights Islands, that I told Jan, Brady and Karla of a most unusual experience (little knowing how much it was to change our lives).

Along with biologists Barry Russell and Tony Ayling and two other companions, Cathy Drew and Les Grey, we were returning to the mainland in my runabout when we met up with a vast school of bottlenose dolphins, 6 kilometres off Tutukaka Harbour. Our 'deep vee' was bucking over a switchback sea, running so fast we clipped the wave crests, virtually airborne. The five of us were totally exhilarated after the day's diving. Suddenly, there were dolphins ahead of the boat. They raced to meet it, arching from the water as they rose to breathe, making their presence known. I eased the machine to whale speed, and the dolphins adjusted their tails to its pressure wave. They surfed ahead of us, cavorting from port to starboard, rolling on their sides to eye the glassy white hull and its occupants hanging over the bow shouting encouragement and slapping the hull with staccato rhythms. Both species, man and cetacean, had begun games-play.

Looking back, I feel that I acted in a premeditated way. I recall that our fast ride had begun in the cathedral-quiet green twilight of Rikoriko, 'Cave of Echoes', the 25-metre-high dome inside Aorangi, chief of the Poor Knights. We had taken Cathy, the New York photographer, in there to view its vastness and had grown silent as we studied the vaulting roof with delicate ferns clinging to it, marvelling at the dim light they tolerate.

Now, as the dolphins moved to meet our fast-running boat, I knew exactly what I wanted to do when I met dolphins on the bow. I wanted to slow to a crawl, put the boat in a wide circle, and leap into the centre with my camera. I wanted dolphin photos, at this stage with the thought that they would satisfy a publisher's request.

Tony took the wheel and I plunged in. My strategy seemed to work—

dolphins were frolicking around the bow like circus ponies, with me as ringmaster. I fired off my photos, then became aware that roles were changing. The boat had stopped, and I was now at the centre of a cyclone of dolphins. I called to Tony and the others to join me, but one at a time, and 'let's all do the dolphin-kick'.

On island voyages with Dr Walt Starck we had often entered villages where there was a language barrier. To our delight the kids would open up communication through playful mimicry and dance. I now found myself spontaneously behaving in the same way towards this ocean tribe. During our dolphin games, each diver in his sealed-off world became aware that the dolphins were demonstrating new tricks. I was weaving among them with a fluid dolphin drive, my fins undulating together like a broad tail in a movement that began at my head and rippled along my body. A dolphin drew alongside me and made eye contact. By counter-opposing its flippers, like the ailerons of a plane making a spin, it barrel-rolled right in front of my mask. Maintaining the dolphin-kick, I imitated this corkscrew manoeuvre, counter-opposing my hands held close to my chest. The response was slow as my pseudo-flippers were tiny and my speed a fraction of theirs, but I found myself rolling wing over wing. Then something startling happened. The moment my spin was complete, a formation of six dolphins abreast of me and on the same side as before, repeated that trick in unison, reinforcing my newly acquired mimicry pattern. And so it went on, the sea wild with energy, a maelstrom of dolphins, their shrill chorusing whistles dinning in our ears. We gambolled with them for about an hour until utterly exhausted. Then one by one we hauled ourselves in over the stern. Around us we could now see hordes of dolphins leaping singly or in symmetrical pairs for a mile in every direction. We must have met a whole tribe of bottlenose dolphins on their passage along the coast.

As we towelled ourselves warm I commented how marvellous it was that such huge, sharp-toothed animals, each as heavy and as fast as my boat, had not even buffeted us with their swirling movements. 'Only once,' said Tony Ayling who had been last on board. As he was approaching the stern, one dolphin had rushed to within a metre of him and stopped short, vertical in the water, with flippers flung wide as if imploring us to continue. We felt we had let them down. I gave the hull a resounding thump. From a short way off a tail smacked on the surface in answer. I thumped again. Eight times we exchanged signals, and that was it.

For the next year I devoured every written word I could find on dolphins and whales. Knowledge of dolphins, I found, was based almost entirely on captive animals. How much could be learnt about our species from a study of people in prison? Jane Goodall had shown what could be done through behavioural fieldwork with wild dogs and chimpanzees and proved that much more could be learnt about these creatures when they were studied in their natural surroundings. But gaining acceptance of terrestrial mammals is far easier than with ocean-dwellers.

I discovered that there had been many problems when first attempts were made to communicate with dolphins. Back in 1969 when he wrote *The Dolphin: Cousin to Man*, Robert Stenuit pointed out that wild dolphins refused to associate with man underwater. For the most part, when divers encountered dolphins swimming free in the ocean and attempted to film them, their plans were cut short. The dolphins swam away. In his book *Dolphins*, Jacques Cousteau openly admits defeat in his attempts to study dolphins in the wild. In order to complete a film, Cousteau had to capture dolphins and restrain them in the sea with nets and buoys. In a storm two net-confined dolphins were almost drowned. Cousteau declared he would never again capture dolphins to film them.

Gradually, during this year of library research, my ideas formed a pattern of possibilities to be explored. Could Jan and I take up the challenge those dolphins had offered with their body language and gain some insights into the enigma surrounding them? We had seen a way through the problem that had faced Cousteau, but where would it lead? Was mimicry and play the first step as it had been when we were meeting island people? If we remained passive observers, they would leave after mutual scrutiny. Any advance towards them led to an early departure. But by gaining their interest through interaction we could possibly prolong contact, which would enable us to recognise individuals and begin to understand them. Any study of free-ranging dolphins would have to be on *their* terms. The challenge would be to discover just what those terms might be. If we were sensitive to their behaviour, an interspecies ethical code might emerge.

The charge that it would be anthropomorphic to study dolphins through the use of a communication model seemed absurd to me in view of the approaches those dolphins had already made to us, and because of the problems faced by conventional methods of study. But it would be a strange and unsettling process—a step beyond the scientific model of reality . . . Project Interlock had begun.

2. Dolphin Body Language

The corkscrew manoeuvre and mimicry of that first dolphin encounter provoked me to take body language much further. I had already made a series of behavioural experiments on fishes, using models. I'd found that there are special markings and signal patterns that reef fishes use in courtship, aggressive display and parasite removal (see *Wade Doak's World of New Zealand Fishes*). Certain ritualised movements or dance routines communicate messages between members of the same species and from one species to another. A black angelfish turns its back and extinguishes the white ear marking on its head, to appease a dominant invader of its territory. Many wrasses bear signal flags on their fins, and some have signature markings on their bodies for personal recognition. Coral shrimps wave their six long, white feelers from beneath ledges to attract customers for parasite removal. The sabre-tooth blenny mimics the swimming pattern and coloration of the cleaner wrasse to approach unsuspecting fishes and nip pieces of their skin.

Assuming that dolphins are at least as intelligent as fishes in observing such signals and body language, what would be their response if I were to mimic them in colour, form and movement—to turn myself into a model dolphin? At least they might enjoy the charade, but I hoped they might accept it as an attempted communication from an alien terrestrial mind, perhaps something beyond the limits of cetacean belief.

I reasoned that something must have triggered the intensity of our April interlock and served to prolong the dolphins' interest in us that day beyond all our previous experiences. Perhaps there was some factor in the way it just happened quite spontaneously.

So I decided to take it all one stage further. I would try the same thing but this time the humans would have dorsal fins fitted to their weight belts. They would wear special wetsuits modelled on the dolphin body: black above and white below, both legs enclosed in a sheath of neoprene and terminating in jet-fins or ideally a model rubber tail-fin, with a peduncle keel.

As swimming bipeds we instinctively use an alternating kick, but the sinuous waving of body and tail-fin is a much more effective and widespread mode of water propulsion. Instead of just increasing the power of our kick with rubber fins, why not copy the fish, as the cetaceans have done? Besides, this would be an indication to the dolphins that we too are intelligent observers of convergent evolution and have not permanently overlooked the fish's advantages. Propelled by transverse waves flowing through its musculature, the fish penetrates the sea with minimal disturbances or cavitation—a highly efficient transfer of body energy to wave motion and mass propulsion that the dolphins have emulated.

Midway along the dolphin's body the dorsal fin serves as a keel, providing lateral resistance about which the body can turn or pivot. Its function can be seen when the bow-riders suddenly swerve aside and leave the ship. Such a fin attached to the centre lead weight on my belt might assist dolphin-swimming. Certainly it would help me get the feel of it while watching them. My whole body had to become a swimming organ.

The dolphin's flippers serve as ailerons for rapid diving, ascent and spiral turns. They are also important for touch communication, an essential part of social activity. I would wear a pair of hand-fins made from plywood and covered in foam neoprene. I made a rough mock-up of my concept—just enough to test its practicality for swimming.

Journal, 4 November 1976: For dolphins it would be far easier to move around than remain motionless. I came to this conclusion today when I tested the dorsal fin, hand-flippers and dolphin suit.

On a calm spring day Jan and I boat-bounced 22 kilometres over the southeast swells towards Aorangi, island of the cloud chief. Two puffs of vapour, the only ones in the entire sky, hovered above the Poor Knights. Recent rains had discoloured the sea as far out as 5 kilometres—but the ocean around the islands was sparkling clear, a fresh upwelling after the storm. There were no signs of bird activity apart from huge rafts of petrels bobbing on the swell—the new water was low on plankton life as yet. We cruised around the cliff faces searching for signs of nautilus and anchored for lunch on Landing Bay Pinnacle—opposite Taravana Cave, an ideal place to test the gear.

Getting into the water presented special problems without the use of hands and legs. I set myself up on the stern, steadied my mask with one flipper, and plunged headlong in. The momentum of my fall carried me completely through the surface and I found myself flying around the boat in an effortless arc. Thinking back on it, the sensation was very curious—as if I had left my body. My mind was still, as though contemplating the body's action from afar—like the first time I flew a hang-glider. The dolphin motion was autonomous: I didn't seem to be consciously striving. Maybe some cellular blueprint for undulating movement was triggered by the 'memory' extensions I had made to my form. In a situation where survival would instinctively depend on a kicking action I was a legless monopode. Perhaps the physical suppression of a habitual pattern released some vestigial spermlike wriggling pattern. Because my legs were hobbled I had to move like a dolphin all the time and this forced me to perform better—just as when, dressed in regal garb, an actor assumes the bearing of a king. The one-piece dolphin suit is a makeshift outfit I glued up from neoprene scraps and really needs to be properly tailored to preserve body warmth.

The dorsal-fin keel attached to the centre lead weight of my belt fitted snugly to my body. It made it very easy to move around in curving pathways and stabilised yawing movements, with a consequent saving in energy. The snorkel enabled me to breathe like a dolphin. I was well ballasted and very soon I could glide around just beneath the surface using my new body to rise and descend, turn and twist, like a fish.

But the stinging cold sank in and I found myself losing body heat too rapidly to maintain the pleasurable aspect of the performance. The more I moved, the colder I became—a punishment syndrome that spoilt the previous, and essential, spontaneity of movement. Approaching the boat to climb aboard, I learnt how hard it is to tread water with one leg and no arms.

Lying on my back, I soon warmed up in the midday sun. Pohutukawa blossoms were starting to redden the terraced heights. Like scarlet spears, the blooms of rock lilies, indigenous to these islands, hung from ledges and outcrops. Kingfishers and green parakeets fluttered among the crags, and over every vertical surface sparkling clean forest water was sluicing from recent rains.

Basking in the heat, it occurred to me how the dolphin mind might experience this same calm and tranquillity even while buckling through the sea. Whereas man breathes autonomously and swims by conscious effort, the sea mammal must choose each breath according to the opportunity presented by wave crests and troughs, flashing to the interface for a fleeting lung exchange and curving below to rejoin its companions.

3: The Sound Channel

I hoped that by exploring the potential of body language exchanges in novel ways we might be able to engage the interest of dolphins and prolong contact. But there was another approach I was eager to test.

Sound is something dolphins and humans both experience, most likely in different ways, but there could be some overlap, some mutual aspect, which might transcend the barriers between us. How would dolphins respond to our music if we played them a special recording that demonstrated in analogue manner our knowledge of the frequencies they use? Dr Carl Sagan describes how he set up a visual version of this approach to alien minds aboard the deep-space probe *Viking*.

The frequencies dolphins employ are four and a half times faster than those used by humans. This corresponds to the difference in the speed at which sound travels through water compared with the air. Normal human speech is at the same frequency as all the mechanical sounds in the ocean. To dolphins we may appear both deaf and dumb. But perhaps there was a way to show that we are tuned to the low-frequency sound patterns of music and speech.

I needed a special tape-recording on which dolphin sounds were slowed, stage by stage, to our listening speed and frequency, so that they could appreciate what was going on. Then a piece of Western music would be recorded in stages to four times the speed of normal sound. This would communicate a pattern at their level of perception.

Both man and dolphin are surrounded by an extraordinary chaos of information noise, thousands of bits of data quite irrelevant to survival. The signal-to-noise ratio is low, and it takes complex circuitry for humans to scan incoming signals for pattern. With refined sensory systems, an ability to discriminate between signals and noise becomes increasingly important. Both man and cetacean have evolved as social animals. In a complex social context generating a heavy static of irrelevant noise, selection favoured the group with the big brain, with its bulky cerebral circuitry, noise limiters, fine tuners and pattern-reading apparatus. But therein may lie the tragedy, for when it comes to interlock between minds in media as different as air and water, both parties have missed the bus. Anyway, that was the theory I wished to test.

Then came a meeting with a young Hamilton lawyer, David Harvey. I explained to him that I needed a special tape-recording on which dolphin sounds were slowed to our listening speed, followed by a piece of Western music recorded in stages to four times faster than normal.

To my delight a cassette tape arrived in the mail from Hamilton. David had used two reel-to-reel recording machines to produce exactly what I had outlined. Furthermore, he had put on the remainder of the tape a long recording of humpback whale songs and the vocalisations of 20 different cetaceans. But would we ever get the chance to test it with dolphins? I wondered . . .

4: *Interlocks with Common Dolphins*

Almost a year had elapsed since that initial cavorting with the dolphins—a period when I had been totally absorbed with them, even to the point of trying to adapt my diving pattern to their lives, and we had gone to considerable lengths to prepare ourselves for another encounter.

Journal: 16 November 1976: It was all ticking over in my mind this morning as Jan and I headed the Haines Hunter out of Tutukaka Harbour and wavedanced towards the Poor Knights. The inshore water was green with plankton. To the north of our path a cloud of seabirds hovered, wheeling and plunging into the sea—gannets and petrels working a school of baitfish. We veered over, my heart surging with expectancy. This time in readiness I was wearing my snug-fitting, farmer john wetsuit pants, and all my gear was close at hand.

Dolphins leaping. Common dolphins. *Delphinus delphis.* Our bow was flanked with curving shapes. We slowed and headed towards the school activity. Jan took the wheel while I got the cassette player going: something to interest them, the message tape, side two: cetacean sounds, *Tursiops truncatus.*

The boat circling slowly, we cheered and drummed on the hull while through the fibreglass came the sounds of their big cousins. I was scrambling into my gear—the dorsal fin on my weight belt all set to be donned. The dolphin sounds ended, so we switched over to the song of the humpback whale. I slipped in with the movie rig to record anything odd that happened.

While I was in the water and Jan was steering the boat round me in circles, she could see the dolphins passing me from all sides and knew that I couldn't keep track of them all, my field of vision being so small wearing a mask. She noticed that the dolphins were coming in and riding on the front of the boat for a while; then they would peel off and go back to feeding where the birds were continually plunging in from great heights. Some would then leave the boat to have a look at me, diving under and around me.

There were dolphins weaving everywhere, around me and below—silver-black bullets in the green haze. I could see only 6 metres because of the plankton bloom, but groups of dolphins kept whizzing by within 3 metres of me, twisting on their sides or leaping out of the water and plunging back. When one made a shuddering burst past me, I managed to keep within range of it a while before, just on vanishing point, it whisked around and returned to circle me. From time to time the numbers around me would disperse, and eventually, after about 15 minutes, contact was lost. Jan pointed to the bird activity a few hundred metres away—the dolphins had resumed feeding.

I climbed over the stern and we moved nearer to the feeding frenzy—again the dolphins responded to our presence with frolicsome behaviour, leaps, and tail-slapping. I slipped back in and began diving down and circling about. They seemed to react even more when I descended, but I needed more weight on my belt to do it with ease. The damned camera housing was buoyant.

I was surprised at the frequency with which they were defecating right in front of me. Was it a signal? Dolphins swallow each other's faeces, I had read, but the way the emissions break up in clouds of tiny particles, all they would get is the taste—a form of chemical communication. Did they expect me to respond in the same way? The least I could do was grab at a cloud as if in acceptance of their gesture.

As a dolphin passed me, I heard an extra loud whistle and saw a string of bubbles emerge from its hole just afterwards. I took the snorkel from my mouth and screamed 'ruuaark' at the bunch as they headed directly at me. They veered slightly and passed at close quarters, turning on their sides to eye me as they zipped by.

This session was much longer and more intensive than the first. Jan had stopped the boat and was drifting nearby. It was full interlock in that no other stimulus than my presence was now keeping the dolphins from their feast. The birds working the fish school were some distance away. How I wished I had some companions to reinforce games-play, the exchange of body language. After about 20 minutes the numbers around me diminished. For another ten minutes I played with a pair of the largest in the group, while others came and went sporadically. Were these the oldest in the group? They seemed very curious about my performances with the fin. Whenever I put on a good demonstration of swimming and diving, there was a noticeable surge of vigour. I had improved greatly since practising with rhythmic music. The more I increased my activity, the closer the dolphins came.

I yelled out for Jan to get in, but first she had to make sure she had a rope over the side to hold the boat. As she got ready, two dolphins kept coming over to the boat, looking up at her as they turned on their side and then returned to me.

She was just about to enter when they disappeared. They must have satisfied their curiosity and resumed feeding. I got back in the boat at a quarter to eleven and we headed for the Knights. We didn't measure the time I was actually in the water with them, but the whole period they were in contact was 40 minutes.

About 3 kilometres from the islands a string of leaping dolphins passed us on a parallel and opposite course. Careering along at top speed in a series of arcs like a rippling rope, they took no notice of us.

Homeward bound, after visiting Rikoriko Cave, we were skittering over the crests of a rising easterly sea 18 kilometres out when we saw birds working near the Pinnacles. Closer in, dolphin fins appeared. I'd left my wetsuit on for the return journey, just in case another opportunity arose. It was much quicker this time to approach the dolphins. Our tape was transmitting the humpback song and in no time we were with the nomads again. Out there the water was oceanic blue and the countershading of their bodies looked quite startling against the backdrop.

With the whale sounds playing we approached and I leapt in. One dolphin sprang out and thwacked the water with its tail as he re-entered. He seemed excited at what he heard. There was a baby with its mother. The mother leapt out of the water and there beside her in mid-air was the baby, only about 60 centimetres long, a miniature version of its parent.

It was incredible to think that such a tiny thing could not only keep up with the speed of its mother, swerving and diving in perfect time, but it could leap out of the water at the same level as its mother too. It seemed to be glued in place by two invisible rods. Its position beside her never altered a fraction as far as I could see.

Jan was circling me in the water with the boat, yelling over and over 'Too much! Too much!' as she watched the activity around me and knew I must be out of my mind. From the boat she had a much better view of how many dolphins there were. She could see them circling me at times when I couldn't. She was not sure whether it was the same ones that kept going back to the feeding frenzy and then returning to circle me or ride on the bow wave or whether they were different dolphins each time.

In the end there was no need to keep the motor going to attract them. They were coming in anyway and seemed very curious about my dorsal fin. Down below I found the schoolfish activity was frenetic: a white line of foam zipped across the surface hotly pursued by birds and crisscrossed by dolphin fins. The hunters seemed to be divided between me and their quarry. I felt honoured at the attention they gave but was not surprised when they hurtled back towards the melee only to return for another series of circuits.

After 15 minutes of such antics I left them to it. I felt I was encroaching. What creature would abandon a high feast to play games as they had done? Schoolfish activity had been very lean that season with all the lousy weather and low temperatures (only 15° Celsius inshore this week). I was glad the dolphins were having such a picnic.

22 November 1976: One week later we met the dolphins again. This time Jan had her first experience of playing with them, and Claude, our neighbour, did too. On another day of calm, a brief break in the weather following a southeasterly blow, we set out for the offshore islands, hopeful that the stormy weather might have brought the nautilus in. The ocean seemed deserted—there were no signs of activity until we were within 5 kilometres of the Knights. Then to the north of our course we sighted gannets wheeling and plummeting. We homed in on dolphin fins. Soon they were gambolling around our bow. While the boat circled I leapt over wearing the dolphin fin. The tape was playing dolphin sounds (*Tursiops*) at half normal speed, decreasing exponentially until they were as slow as human vocalisations. Once I was accepted, Claude joined me. We tried to stay together in a pair like the dolphins, but it was difficult to match their synchronised swimming.

With my Pentax camera and 35 mm lens I was trying to get pictures of the group in the hope that we might find body marks and scratches from which to recognise them in future encounters. I noticed one with an oval white marking in front of its dorsal: White Patch. The concentration on taking photos wrecked my relationship with the dolphins. Squinting through the viewfinder and adjusting the aperture, I lost the spontaneity of play and failed to respond to many of the cues they offered, the body-language gestures that, if I took the trouble to imitate them, heightened their excitement and demonstrativeness.

Claude decided to slip on his aqualung. Perhaps because of my camera the dolphins' attention had turned more towards the boat than me. As it cruised around slowly I could see Claude 12 metres below and 90 metres above the sea-bed, the centre of a dolphin circus. Later he told me he agreed about the faeces signal. It was a definite gesture, he felt. From down there he had a three-dimensional uninterrupted view of the situation compared with a surface-oriented snorkeler. He saw two dolphins peel off from bow-riding and spiral down to his level. At distances of 3 and 4 metres respectively they both released faecal clouds and rejoined the group.

Claude and I were exhausted after 45 minutes' frenzied activity. We climbed out. The dolphins resumed feeding nearby. We were adrift with the music playing and Jan was getting into her gear when over the calm sea came what seemed to be the entire tribe—some 30 or more dolphins, lolling about slowly in groups, a playful indirect movement towards the boat about which they sported, occasionally lifting their heads out of the water briefly.

Jan hurried into her gear and leapt in. They were immediately all around her. She didn't know how many there were altogether but was mainly conscious of a group of five that stayed with her.

She dived down and dolphin-kicked. Straight away they mimicked her with exaggerated movements. She couldn't believe her eyes. This was the first time she'd been in the water with dolphins. Surfacing, she stuttered with excitement to us in the boat and then took a deep breath and dived down. Again she did the dolphin-kick and again they responded with an exaggerated version. Round and round they circled. There were two pairs and a single one. Every time it was the loner, perhaps lacking a mate, that came closest. She extended her arm and it seemed less than a metre away from her outstretched fingers.

The dolphin wagged his head at her and seemed to want her to dive deep and follow his antics. She had to go up for a breath for the next dive. She could see them faintly far below, their white undersides flashing as they turned, so she knew they were still there. As she dived again five dolphins came hurtling up from the depths like spaceships taking off, with all their noses pointed straight at her. It was a cylinder of dolphins. They were close together, almost touching. Just before they reached her they peeled off. The pairs reformed and the loner spun around her very closely, defecating as he swept past with his exaggerated dolphin-kick and wagging head. She rolled over and over. One couple slapped each other with their fins and then let out a shower of faeces as they streamed past her. They seemed to want her to copy them. She felt they were disappointed because she had to keep breaking off for air and was unable to dive deep. So it went on for half an hour; every time she descended they would come rushing up vertically to frolic around her.

These dolphins came in of their own accord. The boat was not running to attract them. When they arrived the music was playing and nobody was in the water. That lone dolphin has stuck in Jan's mind very clearly. He seemed to want her to be his playmate, and she will never forget looking into his eye as he made his slow, close passes. 'It was a friendly, intelligent look; understanding, playful and wise all at once.' All the time she was conscious of other dolphins circling at a distance. Towards the end of her dive she played with the dolphins just under the bow of the boat so we could see what was going on. Then she began to feel seasick and it impaired her performance—most frustrating for her! All she had wanted to do was forget everything and swim away with the dolphins, copying all their actions.

Meeting White Patch Again

Journal: 3 December 1976: Today, off the northern end of the Poor Knights, we fell in with a huge band of dorsal fins. This time it was Jan's turn. She leapt over with the thought in mind of meeting White Patch again, while wearing the dorsal fin. This was a really big group of dolphins, but by the time she was in most of them had left to go on feeding. Five stayed close while a few others circled on the outskirts of vision. Among them was a mother and baby who inspected her three or four times then went away to join the rest.

Since she was on the surface, the five that stayed were beneath her and tilted their noses up to scrutinise her. To her delight one of them was White Patch—an unmistakable white circle just behind his blowhole and in front of his dorsal fin. It resembled a watermark, and she wondered how he came to get it there. Maybe dolphins have birthmarks like us. She yelled to me that she had seen White Patch.

The interlock lasted ten minutes. The wind had come up and it was getting very rough. We stowed all the gear very carefully and bucketed off home.

As the boat skittered towards the coast I had time to think things over. White Patch. It now seems likely we have been meeting the same group of dolphins. Close study of individual markings will enable us to recognise each group and to determine whether we are building up a relationship through time.

The hand-fins. Trying them out for the first time amid dolphins I had really discovered how to use them. They control turns to the left or right and enable the dolphins to descend or rise.

The fish has a rudder for turns. So has a submarine, but the dolphin doesn't need one. His flippers enable him to turn with incredible rapidity about the fulcrum of his dorsal—he just points both limbs in the direction he wants to turn and, zowee, he pivots like a jet boat. His body and tail fluke are transfused with a flowing S-bend of energy, but it is the flippers that initiate the manoeuvre, deflecting him up or down, firing him completely out of the water in a high-speed leap or corkscrewing down into the planktonic dark.

We Are Not Alone

Around this time we obtained from the Canadian Embassy a film, *We Call Them Killers*, that affected us deeply. Midway through the film, after two captive orca have demonstrated their physical prowess with leaps and graceful manoeuvrings, biologist Dr Paul Spong appears at the pool's edge. Placing his head between the gaping jaws of the 5-metre mammal, he says, 'Fear is one of the principal barriers that exists between us, human beings, and them, the killer whales. I feel and sense from my own experience that I know the greatest rapport with whales when I'm least afraid of them. When a person places his head in the mouth of a whale he's saying to a whale, 'Look, here I am. I trust you.'

Stroking its head with a yellow feather: 'Killer whales have obviously got highly developed sensory systems in a number of modalities. Their sense of touch is well developed. They're capable of sensing the presence of very small, very fine touches. Like the touch of a feather, for example. They seem to derive some reward from sensory experiences.

'Visual, touch and auditory or acoustic. They have basically the same senses that we do. The emphasis is different.

'We're predominantly visual creatures. Vision, so important to us, takes second place. With them the emphasis is reversed. Hearing is the primary sense, vision is secondary.'

He rubs the rim of a wine glass to elicit a delicate humming sound. The orca hovers close by and lolls about in seeming ecstasy.

'Cetaceans have the most marvellous hearing systems that there are on the planet. Their hearing is exquisite. Ours is good, theirs is exquisite'.

On a poolside movie screen a Native American dances in full regalia—the orca watch. The camera zooms into soft and sentient eyes. 'Their vision is quite well developed. They see about as well underwater, for example, as a cat sees in air, although I doubt whether vision is of that great importance to them, living in the ocean. But we still know, I really feel, practically nothing about the creatures.'

As the film shows Paul Spong in a wetsuit, climbing onto an orca's back, his voice-over says, 'I really don't know what the possibilities are for exploring interspecies communication at the level of physical interaction. But I feel that this is a necessary step in the process. When I'm in the air, in my environment, presenting myself to a killer whale, I'm presenting a rather limited aspect of myself. I always, for example, have the possibility of withdrawing from the situation. But if I'm in the water with them, then they are in total control of the situation.'

He is carried around the pool on the whale's back. In the later part of the film the flautist Paul Horn sits at the pool's edge and begins to play. (No words at first.) Spong comments:

'Sound is something that we certainly both experience and presumably mutually appreciate. Music more specifically is something that we know transcends language barriers in our own species. I see no reason why we shouldn't explore the possibility that it may transcend interspecies barriers. The more a musician can project himself into his music, the more responsive the whale is. Paul Horn, of course, is a fantastic musician—a fantastic person—and the whales, I'm sure, appreciate him in both areas.'

As Paul Horn plays, the orca experiments with its blowhole, attempting to imitate the flute, on the indrawn breath. The film closes with extraordinary close-up shots of the blowhole, which exhibits all the expressiveness of a troubled brow. Eventually it masters airborne sound-making, but the notes bear little resemblance to the flute.

Paul's final comment: 'If there were a process begun in which killers that have been in captivity for five years were released back in the ocean in the same area that they were captured, I think this would be a totally positive step in the direction of real interspecies relationships and understanding.'

Testing the Sound Channel

Several more interlocks with the common dolphins ensued, each teaching us a little more, but the most momentous was at the very end of January.

31 January 1977: The midsummer ocean was so calm. Eight kilometres offshore the only sound was the distant rumble of holiday traffic. Our runabout drifted over a translucent plain. The tape of the whale songs had played right through.

Bob Feigel let out another shrill whistle. The dolphins we'd been following were moving off now. They were working about a kilometre to the south. We found ourselves listening to their breathing and splashing sounds. Then it happened. Our ears thrilled to a raspy, hollow whistle—it came from amid the dolphins. One had answered Bob. I saw a large dolphin surge off to the west. It sounded and emerged, whistled boldly and dived. We were hanging there, Jan, myself and the two girls. And Bob was standing at the grab-rail, whistling across the water and listening to the responses, hardly believing each time that it was not one of us—that a sea creature was making such sounds. Our experiments had taken an unexpected turn.

From the outset it had been the most perfect day—not a breath of wind, the sky a cobalt blue to match the sea, and the water so very clear. Boats everywhere.

Halfway to the Knights with an American writer, Bob Feigel, Karla and her friend Lisa aboard we had met the dolphins at 10.25. This time there were no birds working. One or two gannets and shearwaters were sitting around on the ocean and occasionally taking off for a few circuits.

Jan donned her gear. We cruised along with the dolphins and they seemed very interested in the boat. We had whale sounds playing on the tape and the girls were ringing the cowbell. Just before Jan got in, the small group of dolphins we were cruising with joined up with a larger school. Bob climbed up onto the bow and was leaning over close to the water. It was time to leap in: the dolphins were all around us. As Jan hit the water and dived down dolphins came from all directions to have a look at her, sweeping in to within 3 metres. She dolphin-kicked energetically until she had to ascend for a breath. There were dolphins on the surface only 3 metres away. She dived again and they came in, circled once and withdrew. She could hear their sonar whistles all round when she was below. They were curious but didn't try to mimic her as on other occasions: once they had satisfied their curiosity they left. From examining body marks and dorsal fins it seemed this was a different group from any we had met before.

The second time Jan got in with them was much the same as the first. They had a look at her twice before rejoining the rest of the group. It seemed that only some of the group would ride on the boat and check us out while the majority kept apart, possibly with the school of fish they were working. On every occasion that we have followed common dolphins this same thing has been apparent.

A large launch cruised past quite close. Two dolphins tore in to have a quick look at Jan. The dolphins did not go over to this boat to frolic on the bow wave as might be expected. Yet our boat was stationary with the motor off.

We caught up with them. I got in this time and shot some 16 mm movie footage before they left.

I took some movie of Jan dolphin-kicking with the fin on and some of the boat approaching me in the water with the kids hanging over the bow. Then I made four more attempts to approach the dolphins with Jan and camera, but they sounded and came up further away each time. We wondered if the boat motor drove the schoolfish they were herding deeper as we approached. It was 11.40. We had been moving with them for an hour and 50 minutes so far and we weren't getting anywhere. By this time we were sure this was a new group of dolphins. We decided to try a different approach, starting again from scratch to establish trust.

The taped dolphin sounds finished and Pink Floyd started. At twice the normal speed 'Echoes' (an electronic mimicry of whale song) has a crazy carnival rhythm. Somehow it sounds just right in that setting, and the dolphins all around us showed clearly they were listening to the tape: when the tempo increased a surge went through them and they began to frolic.

I never thought when David Harvey and I first tried that tape one winter's day on the coast, six months back, that we would ever manage to play the entire experiment to a group of dolphins and feel certain they heard the sequence of acoustic logic it expresses. From the outset David and I had hoped that if dolphins ever heard these experiments they might realise that the communication barrier between man and dolphin is the great gulf between the wave bands which each species uses. We hoped there might be some significant response if ever they grasped the analogue message on our tape. So I was particularly interested in this quickening of pace with the Pink Floyd piece. They definitely responded to its jingly, dancing music—a festive mood was induced in dolphin and man. I felt as if we were in a Mardi Gras procession. Bob was driving sedately, letting the dolphins lead us. When the humpback song came through the tape he began whistling the same whistle over and over again, mimicking the whale sounds. The dolphins were all round the boat, riding the bow, rolling over and looking up at the girls. Every now and again one would leap out of the water. It was so clear you could see every mark and scratch on their backs. We started to note in our minds things that we would be able to recognise at another time.

There was one with the top of its dorsal bent right over: Bentfin; another with a nick out of the top of his dorsal: Nicky; another with a nick out of the lower part; one with two grill patches on its left side in front of and behind the dorsal; one with a diagonal scratch on the left side in front of its dorsal.

I saw one roll over on top of another as it went to get in front of the boat. I've never seen them actually touch like that before.

A rush of understanding: of course, every time we meet a new group of dolphins we have to start from the beginning and let them get used to us first. They seem to accept us as long as we are responsive. We must let the dolphins lead us and not the other way round. A new ethic: they are teaching us the rules.

They sped up and Bob altered our pace to keep with them—another knot, letting out a shrill whistle as he did so.

Lisa said, 'They made a whistle back!'

It was then we could hear the sonar peewees even above the boat motor. We had been cruising with them in this manner for 25 minutes.

Dolphins in captivity have been trained to whistle with their blowholes, but for a dolphin to attempt this in the wild was just too exciting for words. By now the dolphins were at quite some distance, but we continued to drift, silently listening, while Bob kept up his whistling. Then we noticed they were getting closer. While Bob whistled they came nosing through the clear water right back to us, defecating as they went, hurtling under and around the boat. It seemed Bob's whistle had drawn them to us again. One group stayed closed to the boat while others spread out around.

We were looking at the group of dolphins ahead when Jan suddenly stopped jotting down notes. She felt as though she had been interrupted. She turned and her gaze joined ours. At that moment out of the water shot a large dolphin. A trio were travelling north very fast to join those ahead that we were concentrating on. As they approached the others we heard two more whistles. Both Bob and I felt this strange premonition too—that something was going to happen. We were all looking in the same direction just as that dolphin broke the water, whistled and plunged back in.

It was now 1.25 p.m. We started up again. While we circled Bob was leaning over the bow with his arm outstretched over the dolphins' backs riding on the bow, whistling to them gently. I saw one answer Bob 3 metres from the boat. Bob touched one, lightly rubbing his fingers along its side. He said afterwards that he was amazed at the softness of its skin. The dolphin gave a start, splashing water with its tail. It came back up again, rolling on its side to look at Bob, then it did a sideways wriggle.

We kept cruising with them in this manner until 1.50 p.m., heading towards the Pinnacles now. Each time we caught up with the dolphins we had whale sounds playing and would ring the cowbell. We wanted them to recognise and get to know us by introducing ourselves the same way every time. Then we would turn everything off and let Bob whistle.

We decided to try getting in with them again. I manoeuvred the boat until we were in front of them. Jan leapt in three times while I kept the boat circling. Much the same thing happened as in the morning. They went away after she had dived down twice, but both times as she dived they came and circled and had a good look within a range of 3–5 metres. The second time one swept in close to about 2 metres and then went away.

They were moving faster by this time in a southeasterly direction, so we decided we couldn't afford the fuel to follow them any more, even though we wanted to. We took off to the Knights, and as we detoured to pass near the Sugarloaf we noticed a fin in the water. Preparing to leap in, we slowed down and circled. It turned out to be a magnificent mako shark. The water being so clear, we were able to see him very well. We watched for a while and then he swam off into the light. He looked tremendous as the sun lit up his huge blue-grey form. We could even see the gills opening and closing on his side. I had almost joined him! Mako sharks are deep-water animals, and we were lucky to have seen it so close.

That night we all slept with dolphins before our eyes.

Thinking Things Over

At this time of year the common dolphins seem to be hunting bait fish where they feed on plankton along current interfaces and thermoclines. One factor in trying to interpret their manoeuvres is that in many instances only about half the dolphins would be surfacing at one time. Very often, it seems, there would be one group swimming near the surface while others spent longer periods submerged. The surface swimmers may be more available for play as some can be spared from fish-tending. They may even be detailed to distract the boat by playing on its bow. The surface swimmers are often younger ones and mothers with babies.

When we approach a dolphin group with a fish school under surveillance, they often sound. This may be because we frighten the schoolfish, which they must then pursue and round up. *We must avoid this in future.* Another ethic.

Dolphins rounding up prey: One method seems to be to form a long line, which may then divide into three groups. I can visualise them driving the fish at five knots and then suddenly sending down three groups beneath the school to completely surround it. The preyfish form a 'meat ball'. Those dolphins on the surface rush together to close the gaps, and feeding may occur.

Vocal mimicry—key to first stage of communication: Vocal mimicry is the first stage in communication between mother and child. The dolphins have now shown they can adapt to our low-frequency airborne-sound signals with perfection. Physiologically it is not easy—a highly consummate feat by an acoustic gymnast. But once the actual production of such sounds was mastered they rapidly perfected their modelling—like a man first learning to make a sound on a trumpet and then playing a recognisable tune.

In captivity it took scientists weeks of reward/punishment training to elicit airborne sounds from bottlenose dolphins. But these were lonely, touch-starved creatures with little choice other than to comply with the research pattern imposed on them. In the wild the dolphins have the trump hand—they can withdraw at will; in this situation people can only proffer themselves to be taught by the dolphins.

Our message tape is a logical acoustic statement. It may act as a Rosetta stone, or a bridge between two acoustic cultures whole wavebands apart. I don't think the dolphins regard us as particularly interesting yet. We offer little diversity of behaviour. Our canned music can't communicate because the element of response is missing.

'OK—you're making cetacean sounds but that's no more intelligent than the wind whistling over wave crests if you don't respond to us.'

First the tape establishes the concept of changing speeds through the four-stage recording of dolphin sounds, slower and slower until their whistle calls become much more complex to the human ear than the shrill whistles we hear normally. Next, a piece of Western music that incorporates imitation whale sounds is presented at increasing speed until it becomes, to us, musical nonsense. Then the humpback whale songs start and Feigel begins to copy the whales. 'That's it,' the dolphins may think, 'humans make meaningful sounds in air, at low frequencies. Let's try them out.' (Maybe they tried for some time but we didn't notice until the motor stopped.) They pucker their blowholes experimentally, sometimes a bit too tight and the air is released in explosive clicks. Too loose, and they make a hoarse, rasping sound. Then they get it right and manage to whistle in air instead of the high-pitched calls they generate inside their heads. We respond with more whistles, but it's hard to show them a patterned performance as yet because they're not on the surface long enough to hear a series of calls. I had the uncanny feeling they must have known when Feigel whistled, because immediately after, one leapt out and responded, but this was just a hunch.

At first we'd tried hard to engage them in the water. Each time we dropped a diver in they made a turn about him and left. Perhaps the preyfish school had been frightened and had to be overtaken. But once we motored along quietly at the same speed as the dolphins we got our first lesson. Bob had begun to notice certain signals that seemed to indicate which way the group would veer. It was this that enabled him to anticipate their turns and so keep right up with them. As long as we did this, dolphins that were surface swimming came close around the boat and cavorted on the bow wave. They responded to changes of pace in our tape and inspected us closely through a mirror-calm surface as they swam in at right angles to the boat.

At these times a wave of happiness seemed to cocoon the whole boat, all its occupants and those below: all moving through the same field of sound and light, the whale songs and the summer's day. I'd kept wondering whether I should get in but didn't want to spoil what was developing between Feigel and the dolphins. I'm glad I had the sense to refrain or otherwise we may not have learnt anything new that day. The dolphins showed us their hunting patterns, they inspected us closely alongside the bow, and displayed a range of antics indicative of joy and exuberance. Even while the motor was going we heard some very loud sonar whistles that penetrated the boat's hull. These may have been earlier efforts to communicate before attempting the airborne sounds.

The dolphins have whistled to us on a fine summer's day. The eerie sounds still echo in my thoughts—the most uncanny and haunting I've ever heard—something alien, droll and utterly perfect—a comforting response from a mind in the sea—an assurance that we are not alone, that bridges can be built and both sides can cross them.

I recalled seeing a movie about hill tribesmen in New Guinea. When gifts were left on the track, they emerged from the jungle, unaware of a telephoto lens, gathered up the parcels, and hurled them down the path. Mutual respect and game-sharing, self-effacement and flexibility are all essential for transcultural exchanges. We may be on the brink of something exciting if we develop a flexible, creative approach.

When we meet a group, if they respond to the boat manoeuvres by following around in a circle, they are amenable to further interlock in the water. But if they only play on the bow when we head along their course, they cannot be induced to stay and play.

5: Interval: A New Approach

The Anniversary Day experience brought things to a climax for the Doak family. From that time we began to face the need for a major change in our set-up. A total commitment of all our resources to the dolphin project was needed if we were to get any further, even if this meant selling up all our negotiable possessions: the Haines Hunter runabout, the utility wagon, and even our Matapouri home. Jan was as convinced as I was: we could never rest now unless we devoted all we had to answering the questions suggested by the first phase of our study.

It was in May 1977 that I wrote a letter to Dr Walt Starck explaining the changes in our situation.

'We've sold the Haines Hunter and ute and bought with the results a 36-foot Polynesian-style catamaran (James Wharram design, fibreglass on marine ply) and a Volkswagen Kombie of ancient vintage but sound in chassis and kind on fuel. To get further into this dolphin project, it seemed essential to make some major changes. Running costs on the Haines were outrageous, and even then we would have liked to have had much more time at sea.

'The more I thought on it, the more the catamaran format seemed to be a valuable component in the pattern of experiments we've been following. So now we've got two 36-foot canoes bridged with a slatted deck, 18 feet in beam.

'This catamaran will enable us to do a lot of experimenting in situations impossible with the Haines runabout. When we interlock with a group we'd like to stay with them through the night, keeping up the games-play as long as it can persist—a whole range of exchanges, recording and transmitting sounds, making physical contact, miming and just enjoying things.

'For filming action on the bow the dual set-up is unbeatable. I'd like to try skimming along in a hammock slung between the bows centimetres above water level, where a wider range of interplays would be possible. I feel that deeper communication must start from a position of greater trust where we place ourselves at their mercy and vice versa.

'Next month I'll be taking delivery of a 12-foot Avon pneumatic boat —it will be a perfect tender for the catamaran, fast and flexible, and useful as an auxiliary if our main engine breaks down.

'The catamaran will enable us to take out groups of people, young and old, who want to play with dolphins. I've had watertight fibreglassed boxes made to house on-deck sound gear for musicians, so we can try playing music to the dolphins and see if they'll join in. This is the level of interlock I'm most eager to establish—a fun situation with groups of both species—sound games and physical games through which new avenues for communication might be tested and explored.

'Until we learn to sail we'll have to use the vessel as a motor-cat; she has a new 28-horsepower Mariner outboard.

'Another facility I'd like to have is a good RT so we can keep in touch with the charter boats on dolphin sightings. We decided to call the craft *Interlock* to identify it with the project. On her bows Hal Chapman is painting rondels that depict man and dolphin in the "Yin Yang" symbol. I have a set of big speakers that fit in the bow compartments. Stereo sailing is a superb way to travel—it makes a virtue of moving at a quieter pace, listening to music and wafting along with the world's wind. Puts us in a very receptive state for meeting the dolphins.'

The Dolphin Suit

The interval was a time for fresh assessments and preparations for a better-equipped approach. A proper dolphin suit was designed, and a manufacturer of wetsuits consulted. Alf Dickenson of Moray Industries is a pioneer skindiver who made the first wetsuits on the New Zealand market—and gave me a sample one, when I was a teenager. Alf came up with valuable suggestions as to how a dolphin suit such as I proposed could actually be manufactured. His practical advice resulted in a one-piece wetsuit fitting both Jan and me, with a rear-entry zipper running from waist to hood. Although the suit had separate legs to maintain body warmth, Alf sheathed it with a thin rubber skirt incorporating a panel of white neoprene material especially imported from Britain. This provided us with a contrasty *Delphinus* body pattern. Wire and neoprene were fashioned into flippers. With some aluminium sheet and a pair of fins, I concocted a dolphin tail-fin to complete the outfit.

Journal, August 1977: The catamaran has just been on her maiden voyage as a dolphin research vessel—a trip we've all been planning for months. The process of preparing is complete. The ingenious arrangements Malcolm Pitt put together, the 2-metre by 3-metre stern platform that hinges down into a diving ramp, and the special steering system that gives tight control when people are in the water, have worked like a charm. He says he dreamt it up stage by stage, at night. I feel ashamed of my impatience as I pushed him a bit and will tell him so. I didn't realise how difficult it would be to design a system such as we needed.

Outside the harbour our sailor friend hoisted the mainsail and we headed along the coast towards Ngunguru in a light southwesterly. Then we went about and swooped north again. As wind squalls hit the sails I saw no stress on the rudders—Malcolm could just let her go and roll a cigarette as we knifed through the water. When gusts hit us the catamaran didn't react for a small interval, and then she just surged ahead, with perfectly even keels as if I had pushed the accelerator lever on the deep vee. Now Jan and I must learn to sail—quite a hurdle ahead but sure to be a pleasurable experience.

Journal, 6 October 1977: The first time we met dolphins with the new catamaran they seemed a bit suspicious to start with. I was lying in the bow hammock, wearing the new dolphin suit.

Here they were—one swam a zigzag in front of the hulls, eyeing me, but keeping its distance. Then others came in, keeping quite clear of the hammock. They were also swimming deeper and were very cautious. We wondered if they were scared of the hammock, thinking it was a net. Then they started to come a little closer, even mothers with their babies. Three times Malcolm glided up to them and cut the motor. The first two times they avoided the space between our bows entirely.

Then all of a sudden, as if a decision had been made, they came up from behind us, between the hulls, to the bow. We didn't see them coming because they were underwater. They got really close to me, stayed for a while, then disappeared only to return from nowhere and move alongside me for a closer scrutiny.

Jan wondered if they might think I was a dolphin caught in a net, with the suit on. Twice they seemed to be waiting suspended as we approached, and the fifth time they stayed in front of me much longer. Swimming along on the outside of the hulls, they would cross in front, looking up at me as they did. Mothers and babies were doing the same.

The sixth time as we approached, I decided to try and get in with them, but before the boat had slowed enough for me to slide in, the dolphins had moved on with their fishing and didn't get a look at the new suit.

Dolphin Girl meets Sideband

When Jan first met the dolphins while wearing the dolphin suit their reaction quite exceeded anything we had expected. At the outset jazz musician Eric Kircher and I had approached them with the inflatable.

Journal, 17 November 1977: The dolphins stayed, milling around the boat while Eric sat on the bow and played his flute to them. After showing interest for quite some time they rejoined the hunters. Eric and I set out in the inflatable to get closer without encroaching on the feeding. In their vicinity we cut the motor and drifted. Suddenly the dolphins were all around us and gannets were plummeting through the surface in rapid succession like feathered missiles. One gannet hit the water right in front of Eric's nose. He looked at me questioningly but I was sure from past observation that gannets were much too adroit to hit us.

When the feeding frenzy ceased, probably because all the prey had been consumed, Eric began to play his flute. Jan could see the dolphin fins crowding around the inflatable. She struggled into the dolphin suit—just in case. I returned to the ship and picked her up. She finds the inflatable much easier to work from when she has the suit on and no legs. She just lies on the side and rolls in very gently.

While Eric played his flute, a group of about two dozen dolphins circled the dolphin girl, inspecting her curiously for 15 minutes as she dived and curved through the sea. After 20 minutes only three dolphins remained, and then just one. The rest resumed their fish-herding occupation with the main group.

The loner was so curious it came within a metre, spiralling slowly. When Jan descended it dived beside her, coming in much closer underwater than on the surface. When she ascended the dolphin rose too. Every now and then it would disappear, but the water was so very green and murky with plankton it didn't have to go more than 5 metres to be beyond her vision. With its sonar the dolphin could easily scan the dolphin girl as it circled in the fog. She knew it was close by as she could hear its sonar whistle calls. Each time she dived, sure enough, into vision it came, circling very slowly.

'It was looking at me with that wonderful eye,' Jan told us. She was quite overcome with emotion to have a creature like this come so close, scrutinising her with such interest over and over again. In these circumstances all she felt she could do was hang there motionless underwater, gazing at the dolphin, taking in every part of its handsome, streamlined form so that she might recognise it again.

She called it Sideband. It had a white vertical band on its left side behind the dorsal fin. It wasn't a scar but looked more like a watermark on a painting. A large dolphin, it was a paler grey than most.

Then she remembered to mimic it. The response amazed her. As soon as she began moving like a dolphin, Sideband responded by throwing its tail up and its head down, performing its own exaggerated version almost to the point of absurdity. Jan wanted to laugh for sheer joy.

Topside on the boat we watched the game with equal delight. You could have bet money on it—every single time that Jan ascended from a dive the dolphin would bob up alongside her, gasp and descend. We knew it had to be circling her out in the murk, because every time she dived it would rejoin her.

After 30 minutes Jan was very tired and she rolled into the inflatable, now tethered to the big boat. She sat there alone, stretched along the side, and to her delight right beside her in the water was Sideband. She extended her hand towards it as the inflatable glided forward under tow.

Her strength recovered when the original dolphin group returned. She slipped in again and dived. There were dolphins everywhere, sweeping beside, under and around her, all defecating as they passed by. She performed a couple of rolls and noticed two dolphins do the same, their white bellies flashing.

After a while the majority withdrew, leaving the same trio: Average White, Smallscar and her special friend, Sideband. It swam along slowly with her, and when she lost it in the murk, she dived. Always it would sweep in close, to surface beside her when she did. There was a definite pattern emerging. When she descended, it always dived at the same time and came in closer to her than when on the surface.

She was unable to know Sideband's sex, because she never caught a glimpse of its underside. It would pass her very close but always on the same level or slightly below. I shot a roll of film of the episode. I was itching to film it underwater, but this might have upset the pattern emerging. Every so often the other dolphins would return for another look.

Twice Jan got out for a rest and each time Sideband swam beside the inflatable. The third time she got back in the water a fourth dolphin had joined the trio: Grillmark, with a grill pattern on its left flank just in front of its dorsal.

By now Jan was beginning to feel exhausted with continual diving and breath-holding. She lasted only ten minutes, and remembers thinking, 'If I black out now, I wonder if this dolphin would come and support me?' She was getting dizzy from staring at the shafts of sunlight shining on the plankton particles, long rays forever angling down into the depths.

The moment Jan decided she would have to get out, unable to return, Sideband disappeared, as if it knew.

The total time this dolphin had bonded with her was 4 hours and 20 minutes. We were sure now that the dolphin suit must have had something to do with this, because we had never had such intense interest before. In fact I have not been able to find any other account of a human/dolphin encounter in the open sea of such duration.

As we cruised homewards at sunset we wondered what would happen if we ever managed to meet the dolphins with more logistics. Could we stay with them all through the night? Would we gain complete acceptance à la Jane Goodall? At least on this occasion it was our side that had terminated the interlock.

Touching

Journal, 18 November 1977: The following day we met the same group of common dolphins and two of them deliberately made contact with us as we dangled our limbs amid the bow-riders. I had noticed that dolphins usually shudder and flee if people touch them unexpectedly, so I decided just to offer myself and leave it to them. While Peter Munro blew his trumpet on the port bow, Malcolm extended his hand, fingers spread, from the starboard bow. A dolphin examined it in detail for some time, turning on its side about 60 centimetres from the hand. I dangled a foot to offer an alternative—another human extremity.

Contact had been initiated by Malcolm, who stroked the back of one that had been swimming close to his hand—it sped aside but not away. At that point he was in the centre of the net by the bell. He later shifted to starboard bow. I watched in sheer delight as the dolphin veered slightly and gave his hand a definite nudge. Shortly after I felt a dorsal fin glide sensuously between my toes. We continued, Malcolm with his hand on the starboard bow, me in the starboard hammock about a metre away.

Shortly afterwards I saw one sidle up to Malcolm's hand and give him another nudge. It was an unmistakable gesture. All the while the humpbacks were singing through the stereo in each bow and Peter was playing his trumpet to dolphins cruising just beneath the surface, half a metre from the bell of his instrument.

During this encounter, each time the dolphins approached us, the first to arrive was Double Nick. When contact was broken, this dolphin clapped his tail on the water very deliberately off our starboard bow. From thereon the dolphins were hunting vigorously. After further attempts at contact we decided they were too busy with a small, fast-moving prey school, so we hoisted sail and blew home on a path south of the Sugarloaf.

Dolphin Girl Again

Journal, 2 January 1978: Several weeks elapsed before Jan had another opportunity to join the dolphins again clad in the dolphin suit. Once more their reception left her deeply moved.

With sweet flute music playing through the bow speakers, we met common dolphins out near the Poor Knights. It has become our practice to establish mutual trust from the outset by lying in the bow hammocks within their reach for some time before entering the water. In this way we are equally vulnerable to each other. Once they show an interest in the music and accept our presence close by, we feel we may enter their space.

Dolphin girl slid out of the net and clung to the leading edge for a while so the dolphins could see her. Two on the starboard bow looked across. She felt the catamaran slow down. She dived. Immediately five dolphins swam around her, moving slowly and showing great interest. She just kept swimming and diving as the dolphins circled, swooping under her, some coming up from behind, some straight towards her or in from the side. She got the feeling she was moving in a set direction. She couldn't tell where, as she didn't want to raise her head from the water and break visual contact with her companions. She became aware that the dolphins were quietly leading her in their direction as she sought to stay with them. She just forgot about everything and became a dolphin.

Then she noticed there was only one dolphin left, a large one with the thickness toward the tail that denotes maturity. On the right side of its dorsal were two small scratches. All the others had departed. This dolphin kept surfacing beside her, sometimes on her left, sometimes on her right. Each time she caught sight of it again she would dive and beside her the dolphin curved its body in a very graceful arc and slid below too. In time with her body waves the dolphin performed a slow-motion, exaggerated version of the dolphin-kick. Was it mimicking her or giving a lesson? Whatever, this was far from the usual behaviour of a dolphin and it was repeated maybe five or six times. Then it would go on ahead and slowly turn to the right or left to look back at her. She got the feeling it wanted her to follow. Then the dolphin would disappear into the haze only to turn and resume its position in front of her. Sometimes it came up behind her. Once it circled her steadily and she circled too, gazing in admiration at its form. She dived and rolled over. The dolphin didn't roll completely but spun on its side flashing its white belly at her. She was not quick enough to discern its sex. Then it took the lead, waggling its head in that slow-motion dolphin curve again.

Jan noticed that each time it came back the period of separation was lengthening. During one of these intervals she suddenly realised she had forgotten the catamaran entirely, being so absorbed by her companion and its antics. She was shocked to find us some 400 metres away and could not believe she had swum so far oblivious of the boat, her own safety—everything. She saw us preparing to leave in the inflatable. With that momentary glance she felt as if a spell that had been binding her were broken.

The lone dolphin returned three more times, and she dived with it repeatedly. Then it just didn't return. She wondered if the dolphin, sensing her distraction and concern, had decided to leave her. Its companions were far away.

6: Interlocks with Bottlenose Dolphins

During 1978 we continued to meet changing groups of common dolphins in the Poor Knights area. Our journals record some of the strangest, most unbelievable experiences of my life. While I did include some of them in my book *Dolphin Dolphin*, I now feel they strain the credulity of anybody who has never experienced anything of this kind with dolphins. They were on a level that Carlos Castenada has termed 'a separate reality', which left Jan and me doubting our own sanity at times. I prefer to omit that material here rather than risk offending those readers who endeavour to maintain the same objective, rational outlook that I used to pride myself on—before those unsettling experiences...

My initial dolphin encounter, back in April 1975, had been with the large bottlenose species, *Tursiops truncatus*. Ever since then we had been studying their smaller cousins, the common dolphins, and had seldom sighted the big dolphins.

Then, in February 1978, we met a trio of bottlenose just as we sailed out of Tutukaka Harbour. We accompanied them south along the coast for several kilometres. One was a distinctively marked dolphin we came to know as 'Busy Bee', who now has quite a history.

The Busy Bee Story

Busy Bee had a tall, thin, white-tipped fin with a tear at the base of the trailing edge like a protruding thumb. It was a huge dolphin and had an air of power about it. We got a good photo of this distinctive fin.

Some time later I met a neighbour with a dolphin story. Bill Shanks was crewing on the fishing-boat *Busy Bee* when it was servicing a huge experimental trap net up at Whale Bay. One morning they found a big dolphin in the net. To release it necessitated hauling the dolphin on board, but it did not resist in the least. They steamed 5 kilometres out, soothing it and pouring water over its skin. When set free it leapt clear of the water and vanished.

Next day, as the *Busy Bee* left Tutukaka Harbour, two dolphins met them off the entrance with a series of superb leaps. One of them they recognised as the dolphin they had liberated the day before: it had a nick made by a rope in the rear base of its dorsal fin. I showed Bill our first bottlenose pictures. That was how we came to name that big dolphin Busy Bee.

After publishing a description of this dolphin in our newsletter, we received a report from skindiver Alan Morrison. He had seen Busy Bee at Great Barrier Island:

'In the evening of 10 January 1979 at the entrance to the small cove on the north side of Rakitu Island off Great Barrier, members of our diving club met three large dolphins. The two big ones were apparently copulating. We snorkeled with them for half an hour. One of the large dolphins had the top of its dorsal missing. Another appears to be your Busy Bee dolphin, and the smaller of the trio has a nick from the tail and a small spot on its dorsal.'

A short while later—on 22 January—we sighted these same dolphins on our stretch of coast, 80 kilometres to the north.

Subsequently the vessel *Busy Bee* was wrecked. The bell was given to R.V. *Interlock*. This is the bell we ring whenever we meet dolphins.

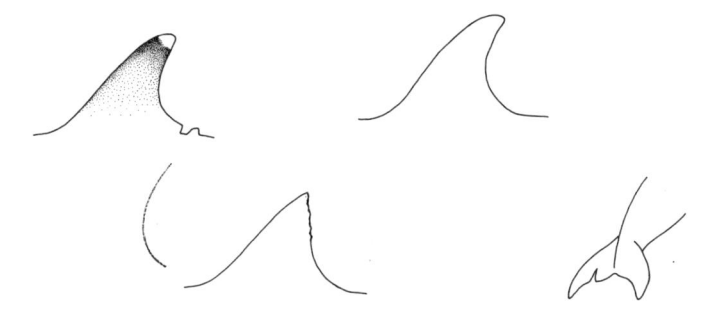

Busy Bee (left) and companions

Follow Home Day

In May, while we were at anchor in Ngunguru Bay on the mainland coast, four bottlenose had approached our catamaran. Jan joined them in the dolphin suit while they swam closer to her in murky conditions and I shot movie footage topside. Then they accompanied our vessel all the way back to Tutukaka. To our surprise they followed us through the entrance. I had the chance to try out an electric 'towpedo' with them.

Jan passed the heavy orange machine down to me. With propeller whirling, at top speed it hauled me under, and I curved around in the twilit harbour, amazed to find schools of kahawai, snapper and parore, stunned in their tracks as I zoomed into view. Then I met the dolphins. They must have heard the whining motor long before, and when they saw me, all four turned on their backs, white sides towards me so they were highly visible in the dark water. In this position they spiralled around in a tight circle.

Veering the towpedo as hard as I could, I followed them around, and we all sped off across the harbour. But they were much faster, and I followed while the catamaran and inflatable trailed me for safety's sake —there were boats everywhere. The dolphins put on a star turn for the boats crowded with tourists, but ignored those with nobody on deck. Quietly they skirted the harbour shores and left through a narrow gap in the rocky entrance, keeping us clear of the busy main channel.

Out around the steep headland we followed, and they began to play on our bows in the setting sun. Graven on my mind-screen are the silhouettes of dolphin fins on beaten copper. Then the dolphins made a gesture we have seen before from *Delphinus* at the end of an interlock: all four in line, they leapt together and slid under in perfect unison. They reappeared and repeated the same manoeuvre. When we got to our moorings there was just sufficient light to secure the ship.

Our next meeting with bottlenose dolphins was like a re-enactment of the 1975 encounter: we met a very large group and they stayed with us as long as we could endure. This was what I call an 'open-ended interlock'.

Nudelock Day

22 January 1979: Tony and Avril Ayling, up here for a science congress, delayed their departure by a day to come to sea with us. Both having completed doctorates in undersea ecology, they were just on the point of leaving for Australia, where they would begin a programme of Barrier Reef research with Dr Walt Starck, aboard *El Torito*.

It meant a lot to me to show these two sea people the kinds of things that have been happening to Jan and me when we meet dolphins with our *Interlock* set-up and to receive an evaluation of our study methods from two trained scientists.

Tony was involved in the initial interlock back in April 1975, when we danced with *Tursiops* for an hour. Since then, although we have had many intensive meetings with *Delphinus*, we have not had an interlock with a large group of *Tursiops* like that—until today. I went over in my mind the *Tursiops* meetings we have experienced: Busy Bee, Stumpfin and Nicktail in February 1978; then in May the four encountered near Goat Island that followed us into Tutukaka Harbour.

On 8 September 1978, Tony Ayling saw a group of *Tursiops* playing courtship games and copulating vigorously in Nursery Cove at the Poor Knights Islands. Tony found it very hard to concentrate on his long-term fish behaviour observations.

A dolphin would swoop above the bubble kelp forest that fringes the

Sand Garden, dive into the top of the fronds, grab a piece in its beak, break it off, swim with it for a while, and then drop it. He saw the seaweed game several times on two separate dives. This links up nicely with what happened today.

This morning at 11.45 Tony thought he saw dolphins leaping a long way to the south. We kept on the same tack and they came to us—all over the ocean, bottlenose dolphins leaping. A tanker heading north along the coast had dolphins shooting from its bow wave. Like torpedoes, several every minute would spurt from the crest of the huge standing wave on the tanker's bulbous forefoot. Just then Eric Wellington, with the charter boat *Southeast*, came alongside us from astern with dolphins on his bow. As he drew away, dolphins were leaping astern of him and in front of us. Then gradually they came to and all around us, some thwacking the water with their tails.

Avril and Tony got into the bow hammocks for an initial short contact. There were many young dolphins at this stage. The dolphins went to Eric and the tanker and then returned, but there were no young ones with them now. This time interlock really began. Tony thought it was not going to happen, but I said I felt confident it would gradually intensify. With just a gentle southwesterly breeze we let the boat steer itself. There were three in the net with masks on. Frenetic activity began around the bows.

'You can see them coming from away off,' yelled Tony, lying in the net, his head submerged. The water was clear, with over 30 metres visibility. The message tape was playing Pink Floyd sped up, and then songs of the humpback whales.

Avril overbalanced and fell in front of the net, so clung there. Brady slowed the boat more and Jan and Tony joined Avril in the water. Tony shot a whole roll of film with his Nikonos and fish-eye lens.

Jan noticed a dolphin with its dorsal damaged at the base, 'Wade, I think Busy Bee is here!'

Just as I looked over to the port bow, a fin thrust into view—it seemed almost deliberate, and with it was a companion with a short stumpy fin. We got out our fin identification file and compared them. It was Busy Bee and its companion Stumpfin, whom we had met and photographed a year before—on 16 February 1978. Recognising them was like seeing old friends.

Jan got out and put on her dolphin suit. Tony suited up too. Avril stayed at the bow to maintain contact. She exclaimed that one opened its mouth, showing its teeth as it passed, but not aggressively. Another would hang vertically in the water, rising slowly as a diver does for a breath. She called it Triplenick.

Jan and Tony re-entered in their wetsuits, the three of them dragging through the water clinging to the bow net, with dolphins converging from all sides and up underneath them from behind, to inspect the humans dangling from the orange net. The dolphin movements got slower and slower, until some were almost motionless around the bows.

Triplenick became excited, dashing about as all three divers swam away from the catamaran. Jan saw a dolphin with a piece of fishing line hanging from its tail. Three times she yelled 'Tepuhi' as the dolphins moved slowly around them close to the surface. She noticed one to the left look directly towards her and let out a huge volley of bubbles like the exhaust from a scuba regulator. It really seemed to mimic her action, but not the sound.

Each time they dived, the dolphins dived also and swept in close, head on, or they would come up behind and curve around in front, less than a metre away. Whenever they came from behind they came closest; Tony said later, 'Closer than I've ever experienced before: 60 centimetres from my body, 15 centimetres from my hand.'

And Jan, 'They were huge—such massive, strong forms moving in front of my eyes. I've been so used to swimming with the smaller pelagic dolphins, *Delphinus*. These *Tursiops* were giants in comparison.'

Triplenick kept paying Jan, in the dolphin suit, a lot of attention. It would sweep around her, exaggerating the dolphin-swim and tossing its head playfully like an exuberant puppy. When she dived, it came in head on, and as she finned horizontally, swam beside her, eyeing her intently. When she rose for a breath, to her amazement it stood vertically in the water and rose up to the surface regarding her as it went. It was so comical she actually laughed. She had the urge to throw her arms around it in a hug. The gesture was repeated several times.

She found later that Tony and Avril saw the same gesture but didn't identify it with Triplenick, although this dolphin appears in several of Tony's pictures. Twice Tony watched a dolphin hang motionless upright in the water just below the surface to sink very slowly, tail first, emitting a small trickle of bubbles. On one occasion it made a slow, yawning gesture. Another dolphin approached him horizontally and hung motionless 3 metres away just looking at him. In 15 encounters with *Tursiops* he had never seen such behaviour.

Jan moved closer to the other divers to see what responses they were having. A large dolphin dived towards her and turned broadside on. Passing 2 metres away, it very slowly opened its mouth twice, open and shut, open and shut. She could see its sharp teeth, but this did not appear to her a threat gesture. For the first time she was able to recognise one dolphin as a male. She was 3 metres below when he swam past her, up-ended and descended with his underside towards her. Clearly she saw the two in-line slits—no mammaries.

Six metres away she saw Avril and Tony together, with Triplenick circling them, then rushing over to her and back around the others, still doing the exaggerated dolphin-swim and tossing its head. She was reminded of a high-spirited teenager. Then she heard the message tape playing. She was near the starboard hull. Whale sounds were floating out and she noticed three dolphins quite close to the hull in a stalled position, just hanging there with their flippers drooping, slightly hunched as if listening to the sounds.

During this time I was operating the hydrophone and the message tape, shooting movie and still, and assisting Brady with the ship. Although bursting to get in with the dolphins, it seemed most important that the two biologists should have the fullest possible experience of our set-up before they went overseas. The message tape was conveying an analogue expression of the frequency we use, paralleled with low-frequency whale sounds.

I heard a dolphin make a blowhole sound in air just as it breached by the bow and surged off at right angles—a loose 'raspberry' sound. Gradually the number of dolphins around the catamaran diminished until only six remained, including Triplenick—two sets of three.

I wanted to film them at close quarters but the cat was drifting south and the dolphins stayed put. As Jan swam to the boat it may have seemed as if she were leaving—she was feeling seasick and tired. Perhaps they sensed this. We were all hungry and in need of a break. Towards the end of this interlock two dolphins came curving in on their sides, and then one made a series of vigorous tail slaps. I replied. We had been together continuously for one and a half hours, our longest interlock ever.

We lunched, drew fin and tail identifications, and sailed on a northerly tack parallel to the coast. Just as we turned east, we saw a pair of dolphins leap high out of the water, forming a neat pattern, like our sail symbol.

They did this three times about 500 metres away. Then at 2.45 several dolphins joined the boat. One of them was Triplenick. This easily recognisable dolphin made three approaches to the starboard bow and then headed off, at right angles, to the southeast. I took photos of the fin. Then, following in that direction, because it seemed like a gesture, we saw lots of dolphins approaching. The second interlock began at 3.05 and lasted an hour. We were about 5 kilometres off Tutukaka, in line with the Pinnacles. This time Jan, Avril and Tony were nude. There were about 50 dolphins, including several youngsters, one so tiny it must have been recently born. About 50 centimetres long, it still had vertical stripes (birth folds) on its sides. Its mother and another dolphin kept it between them.

This time I just had to get in. The ocean was warm, deep blue and clear. I dived down with my 24-millimetre lens, dolphin-kicking, and found I could get 30 dolphins in my viewfinder at a time. Using High

Speed Ektachrome I took some shots at 1/125 f5.6, then 1/250 f4, in case of excessive movement. Jan and Avril looked exquisite with their long hair flowing in rhythm with their dolphin movements.

Afterwards, Avril sent us a painting she had done to celebrate her first dolphin experience—two nude human figures and five nude dolphins. With it she wrote:

'Suddenly there were dolphins all around, big bottlenose dolphins, arriving and flying through the rays of light that shot the deep-blue sea as if it were silk. There were perhaps 60 dolphins, and we felt beckoned to be in there with them. With our bodies naked and trembling with excitement, we repeated their swift movements; effortlessly Jan and I flew with our dolphin-kicks, looking down into the cones of light that swept from our bodies into the darkness below and then around at our partners in this ballet.'

Jan felt the dolphins were scanning her with their sonar at a 5-metre range and then moving in close for visual scrutiny. 'I felt so free, and everything seemed right. We were in our natural state, just as they were.'

She counted 17 and then lost track. There were babies of all sizes, then others making up, as it were, the whole village family. She saw one huge old dolphin, very dark with mottled grey blotches—and one peculiar individual with a 'punched' snout like a bulldog.

Tony and Avril were curving in unison like dolphins. Jan and I joined them, perhaps the most sublime moment in all our dolphin days. Avril and Tony held hands and caressed to show our touch responses. The dolphins did likewise, rubbing along each other's side and folding across each other. Trustingly, these dolphins had brought their young to see us and allowed them to come very close.

When three divers were below at once, each was approached in turn, the dolphin heads swivelling to and fro as they scanned the human forms. We are so limited underwater, unable to communicate—completely cut off in spheres of 'self'.

Jan noticed the tiniest baby swim up under its mother and nuzzle her underside to suckle. Meanwhile another dolphin (auntie?) came up under the baby, gently rubbing it and holding it securely between the mother and itself. Then, as the baby resumed its position beside the mother, it was flanked by the other dolphin, the two adults rubbing their sides against the baby, as if cuddling it. I took a picture of them. I am usually reluctant to use my camera when we meet dolphins, as I feel like a tourist in a village. But, with the second meeting, I felt we were accepted. The dolphin pictures Tony and I got that day are the best I've seen of bottlenose in the open ocean.

Seaweed/Simo: I noticed a dark dolphin with a strand of worn-looking bubble kelp wrapped round its forehead. It came past again on the same level and course with the kelp draped around one flipper. Each time the pattern of approach—course, level and distance—were the same. A gesture.

Jan saw this same dolphin earlier with the kelp draped around the dorsal and, later, around its caudal peduncle. Tony saw it with the seaweed in its mouth when down deep, and around a tail fluke when near the surface. But *nobody* saw it change the position of the seaweed.

By this time I was alone in the water. Out of the midst of the dolphins came a strange shape—a large bronze whaler shark. My first reaction—is there any danger? I looked at the dolphins cavorting with their young. They showed no fear at all. A calm feeling flowed into me. I took a shot of the shark as it cruised past, eyeing me and swimming to the southeast away from us all. (I have also seen a large hammerhead shark swimming with common dolphins who showed no concern, but have an anecdote of bottlenose dolphins attacking a mako and killing it in 15 minutes, tossing its body clear of the water.) My film was finished. I gave Brady the camera and got a beach ball, tossing it to Tony over the water. But the ball is a surface thing. We need something more submersible, a slow-rising buoyant thing like the seaweed—a bit of nylon rope?—to start an exchange game. While Tony and I were tossing the ball, we didn't notice, Jan says, a dolphin leap out alongside us.

As I think back over the kaleidoscope of activity that I observed, several significant things emerge. I recall the photo I took of a large dolphin with a white mark on its jaw. At closer range I saw its beak had been deformed as if from impact. It looked like a pug dog.

One dolphin defecated in front of me. With *Delphinus,* we think this may be a gesture. I swam down through the cloud as it swerved around and watched me. Another two dolphins, 2 metres apart, released gulps of air from their blowholes simultaneously after I shouted 'Tepuhi'.

If only I could get a series of pictures or movie sequences of all the special behaviours. In review: Jan noticed that when I entered with the camera the dolphins stayed about 3 metres from me. When they came closer it was from behind. Then suddenly a dolphin would swoop past so close it was hard to fit in the wide-angle lens.

In our second interlock the dolphins moved in large groups rather than as individuals and frequently dived deep. Again it was the humans that withdrew from exhaustion. In sum, the day provided the longest period of intensive interlock we have ever experienced—Avril's first and Tony's best out of about 15 contacts.

For the first time we showed the dolphins both male and female nudes. They saw Tony and Avril caressing. There was the re-meeting with Busy Bee and Stumpfin, the behaviours of Seaweed and Triplenick, the tail-standing breath rises, jaws-open passes, blowhole sounds, bubble-blowing responses, the defecation gesture, close-from-behind approaches, Triplenick's signal approach to the catamaran, farewell tail-slapping, sonar-scrutiny approaches, the mother-child-auntie association, and the shark.

It would be valuable to analyse *all* the pictures Tony and I took underwater, establish all the recognisable body features, and attempt to identify as many individuals as possible ready for future meetings.

We got home at five, under sail, just in time for the Aylings to catch the bus on their journey to Australia. Avril was ecstatic, Tony no less.

As an aftermath, we have since learnt that the following day (Tuesday), at 6 p.m., *Tursiops* were sighted around the entrance to Tutukaka Harbour, and that from Monday to Wednesday a large aggregation of *Tursiops* was observed by fisheries scientist Mike Bradstock, while aboard one of the pair of trawlers working just north of the Chicks in the exact area where we had met the dolphins. He said there were lots of squid there, which, they suspected, the dolphins were feeding on—possibly at night. The trawl caught a lot of John Dory. Mike sent us a superb sequence of photos he took the day following our interlock and in the same area where we had met the dolphins.

Footnote: Some months later when studying the pictures taken that day we discovered that in photographing the dolphin making the defecating gesture I had unwittingly recorded the seaweed dangler, its companion—a triumph as by then I was lamenting that I hadn't taken a shot of Seaweed. On its right side, below the dorsal, it had a distinctive scar: a figure-eight pattern with one loop open and the other filled in with parallel lines—an elaborate tooth raking made by another dolphin.

From this picture and others, we were able to identify the same pair of dolphins close to the camera at both meetings—as if they had been giving us extra-special attention. Photo comparisons also suggest strongly that Seaweed was one of the 'Follow Home Day' quartet. And there is little doubt that our Seaweed is the same bottlenose that Val Walter, the lighthouse keeper's wife, had been meeting each summer for the past five years, the dolphin she called Simo (see next chapter).

Three months later: Sunday 29 April 1979: Just three of us aboard—Jan, myself and veteran diver Mac McCaffery—we were heading south along the coast towards the Hen and Chickens Islands when I thought I saw a dolphin leap, but wasn't sure. In a matter of minutes bottlenose dolphins were making the most spectacular leaps off our bows.

It was during a hard gust and the catamaran was screaming along. The rough water and strong winds didn't seem to worry the dolphins in the least. They were magnificent, completely free and at ease in the rough conditions.

Jan yelled to them, 'We can't get in the water and play with you out here. It's far too rough. We'll see you in on the coast in the shelter of the land.'

Heading straight towards the coast, I decided to play Jan's game and assume that they *did* understand us. Having to handle the boat in rough seas, we didn't recognise any dolphins at this stage. We saw them heading north, then they disappeared. We felt a bit silly, actually sailing *away* from where we last saw the dolphins. However, we carried on towards the coast. Mac began to get into his wetsuit and I did likewise. As we entered the lee, out of rough water, we suddenly saw the dolphins pop up just ahead. This was wonderful. We rang the bell and they came towards us.

They swam on the bow for quite some time. I was on the port bow and Mac on the starboard. Jan was at the tiller and could see our delight. Mac leapt into the net and shortly after yelled that they had gone. Jan replied, 'No they haven't. They are back here with me.'

The stern platform is so low in the water that the dolphins seemed almost on the same level. They were cruising along on their sides looking up at her. She felt a sudden surge of pleasure to have them near again. Two were swimming along beneath the inflatable, upside down. Then Splitfin and Stumpfin surfaced beside her. There were two other smaller dolphins side by side surfacing together. Their fins were identical, with no markings. She glanced behind and saw a dolphin surface. She yelled excitedly to me, 'I think it's Busy Bee.'

I looked back and at that moment the dolphin surfaced again. Sure enough, it *was* Busy Bee. They played around the boat as we went along. Busy Bee has never come close to anyone in the water in all the time we have seen him but always seems to stay around and expose himself long enough for positive recognition.

7: Simo & the Keeper's Wife

Thirty kilometres east of the forest-clad hill on which we live, a lighthouse winks on the horizon. One day I got the urge to write to the keeper of the Mokohinau light to see if anybody out there was interested in dolphins. To my delight a reply, dated 9 July 1979, arrived from the keeper's wife, Val Walter. This developed into a regular exchange, once we discovered we both knew the same bottlenose dolphin, that Val's Simo was our Seaweed...

'I was pleased to receive your letter with regard to sightings of dolphins around the Mokohinaus. Dolphins are my "special" friends. I mean this in the sense of being interested in them as individuals rather than just as a species.

'During the summer of 1976–77 I had several unusual encounters with one particular dolphin and his companion. Due to a problem with sinus and asthma I am unable to dive but nevertheless I did form a sort of communication with my oceanic friend. As you say, we are in one of the best situations for observing these beautiful creatures in their own environment. We have been on this island now for seven years and in the lighthouse service for 21 years.

'About late October or early November 1976 I used to spend many afternoons fishing off a point of the island that juts into Edith Passage. One day I noticed two large bottlenose dolphins approaching quite close inshore. I hurriedly pulled in my line so I wouldn't snag them accidentally. Much to my surprise one continued to within a metre of the rock I was standing on. It was so close I could hear the blow as it exhaled and a curious high-pitched, twittering whistle. I was startled but stood quite still and tried to whistle back through my teeth. I don't know if it heard me or not but I suddenly remembered reading a story when I was young about a Greek boy who whistled up a dolphin that called itself Simo—so I called "Simo! Simo!" as high-pitched as I could, making the "Si" as much like a whistle, as sibilantly as possible.

'The dolphin turned and approached again to within a metre of my rock, rose up on the surface and shook itself, then dived and swam off towards the other one out in the channel. A few days later I was again fishing at the same time and place when the dolphins suddenly appeared together, about 4 metres from me, seemed to observe me for a few moments, and then swam off about their own business. This became, over the summer period, a regular occurrence, the dolphins usually appearing about half an hour after I arrived on the rocks. Sometimes I would go down and whistle and call to no avail, then just as I would be ready to leave, around the corner they'd appear. On several occasions I lay or sat on the point and reached out into the water, and although the one I call Simo came quite often within arm's reach, I hesitated to make a grab in case I scared it off.

'Then one morning in late January 1977, several bottlenose dolphins appeared in our landing bay and put on quite a spectacular display of leaping, chasing and general play. After lunch my husband Ray launched our small boat off the block and we all went out into the bay and joined the dolphins. At first we thought the outboard might frighten them off but, after circling the boat at a distance for a few moments, they came in close and started rather an alarming game. We had stopped the outboard to listen to their chirrups and whistles as they surfaced. Then they started bumping the bottom of the boat in a sort of game of tag. One after the other, about six of them approached rapidly on the surface, dived about two metres from the boat and gave it a sharp bump as they passed beneath. We had a glass box in the boat so we observed them as they passed under us. You can imagine my surprise when one turned, swam slowly up, and stopped. One twinkling brown eye peered back at me through the bottom of the box! I had an almost irresistible urge to hop over the side and join them. Only the fact I was fully clothed stopped me.

'About 20 of them stayed in the bay for the afternoon. We had plenty of time to let the other family take turns with the boat and the children had a wonderful afternoon. At one stage Andrew, one of our young sons, then about seven, was kneeling in the bow of the boat, his hand trailing in the water as we cruised slowly across the bay with dolphins on either side.

'Several times he almost touched one. Then the one I call Simo came very slowly alongside and up under Andrew's hand. For a few moments he held its dorsal fin and then, suddenly, it leapt straight out of the water and came down with a mighty splash! We were all drenched and the children almost hysterical with glee. I am sure it was quite deliberate on Simo's part, for he veered away, rapidly dived, and surfaced alongside the boat with a long trailer of seaweed draped over his beak. Several times he tossed the seaweed towards the boat and caught it again. After three or four hours they tired of our company and went off out to sea.

'The dolphins were here until March 1977, on and off. Sometimes they met our supply ship, *Stella*, between Fanal Island and the Mokohinaus and accompanied her right up to our landing block on her fortnightly trips. We then saw little of them until September-October 1977, when Simo again appeared at my fishing spot.

'By that time we had another assistant-keeper who was a diver—wetsuit and snorkel. One day in December, while he was diving off the landing block, he was suddenly surrounded by five curious dolphins who circled him several times, brushed him and nudged him, as he tried to stay close to the bottom. He said they squeaked and whistled almost constantly underwater and the sound in his head became so unbearable he had to surface. We all wondered whether some action on his part caused concern to the dolphins or if he was just very susceptible to their sonar.

'Like Simo these were bottlenose dolphins, but on occasions we have had common and bottlenose together in the bay at the same time. This was the case last October when the Air Force divers swam with them and saw Simo.

'In October 1978, we had a party of 20 Air Force divers out here on a ten-day underwater mapping expedition, and I discussed this experience of mine with several of the divers. I also showed them photos of "my" dolphin. A couple of days after the conversation a group of about 30 dolphins came into our bay by the landing, and all of the divers had the thrill of swimming and playing with them.

'Three of the divers were certain that one particular dolphin was "my" friend, as it has three very distinctive scars and, from its behaviour, I would say it was the same one.'

'Please, Say Please . . . '

The afternoon of 13 January 1979, Val Walter went down to her favourite fishing spot, a reef that juts into Edith Passage between Burgess Island, where she lived, and the two adjacent islands. (She sent us this narrative on a tape.)

'I was sitting on the end of the reef, pretending to fish, my usual occupation, and whistling "Amazing Grace". You asked if I sing to Simo—well, I whistle more often than sing. As I whistled, I watched the channel towards the north, because that's the direction the dolphins generally come from.

'On that day Simo must have come from the south, towards Little Barrier Island, because he surfaced behind me about 2 metres away. I heard that soft phphew, puffing noise, of a dolphin exhaling and turned around. Just then a little breeze picked up the small hand towel I used to wipe my baity hands and whirled it into the water, landing close to Simo.

'I said something like "blast" or "bother" and jumped up, grabbed my fishing rod, and tried to get the towel. It did go through my mind that Simo might pick it up like he does seaweed and toss it back to me, but he didn't. He backed off very smartly and watched me, from a metre away, trying to fish up the towel. It floated beyond my reach but was still on top of the water. As it drifted away he moved towards it, but lost interest when it started to sink.

'He came back and reared up out of the water at the end of the reef, looking at me and making funny little noises, like a Pekingese puppy—"Yip, Yip, Yip." I felt he was saying, "Well, what use was it anyway? What did you want the darned thing for?"

'I laughed at him. As often happens when he's done something to make me laugh, he reacted by thrusting his head out of the water and wagging it from side to side—quite comical. But that was the first time he has ever made that funny noise.

'Then I noticed he had a couple of companions out in the channel, cruising up and down, as if waiting for him. I felt they wanted to go so I said, "Well, don't let me keep you here, Simo. Just come and see me next time you're passing." For all the world you'd swear he understood. He just dived and joined them in the channel. Then all three leapt clear of the water, one above the other in the most beautiful arch, all facing north, and landed back with a mighty splash to swim away to the north.

'Apart from a couple of sightings of bottlenose dolphins from the lighthouse, that's the last time of actually speaking to Simo (October 1979). Perhaps it seems strange to talk to him just as you would another human being, but after meeting him many times I feel he *is* just another being, a friend, and that's the way I address him.'

(Nine days later Jan and I met Simo to the north; see page 54).

Footnote: In early December 1979 American film-maker Dick Massey met five bottlenose dolphins between the Mokohinaus and the Poor Knights. He was amazed to find the dolphins came right up to him and he was able to film full-face close-ups of one individual with a distinct scar on its side, 'shaped like a human foot'. Comparison with photos proved this *was* Simo.

Part Two: New Zealand Dolphin Swimming Locations

'If there is magic on this planet, it is contained in water.'

—Loren Eisely

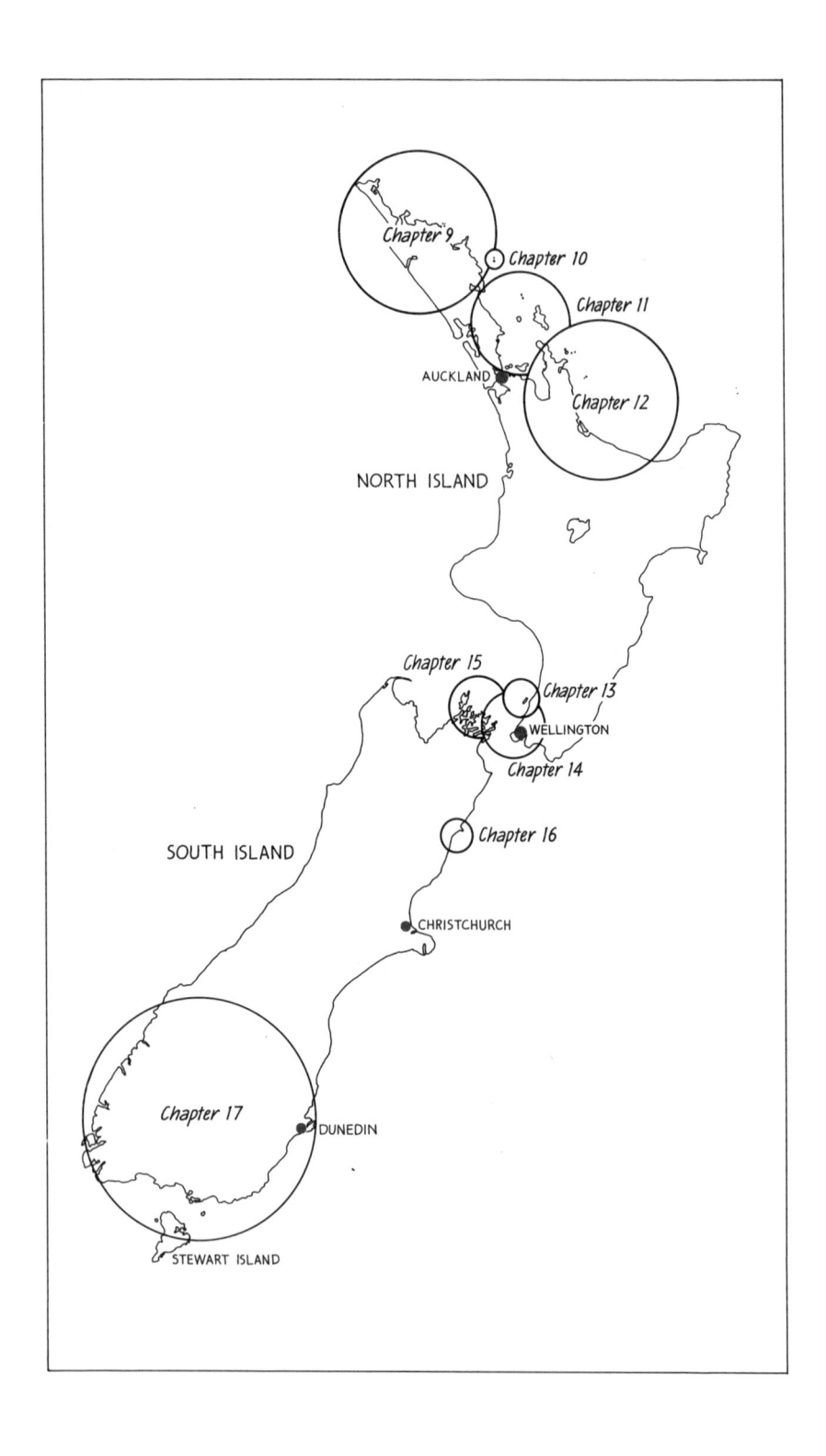

8: Project Interlock Extends

Our extensive correspondence with Val Walter led to an outreach: a new phase of Project Interlock. In April 1979 we took a major step in our research. Having established some guidelines for winning acceptance by wild dolphins, Jan and I wondered if it would work for other divers. As an extension of our experiments, how would dolphins elsewhere respond if more and more people met them in a communicative and creative manner? I had published *Dive* magazine for 15 years and gained a pretty good measure of what was commonplace or rare in the diving world. I was confident that diver-dolphin contacts were, for the most part, very brief: just hello-goodbye encounters, with quite a lot of fear on the human side, as people weren't quite sure what to expect.

So in 1979 we began publishing newsletters in Rob Lahood's *New Zealand Dive* magazine, which outlined the procedures we used to establish friendly rapport when meeting dolphins. We then put out a diver-dolphin encounter questionnaire and sought written accounts as well. The response was quite staggering. Interlock reports came in from right around the New Zealand coastline, from Spirits Bay to Foveaux Strait. Then they started to extend across species until we were filing interlocks with bottlenose, common, dusky and Hector's dolphins.

By early 1980 I began to notice a pattern in these reports. Duration seemed to be the only way to evaluate human-dolphin exchanges in the wild. The more interesting and creative the divers, the longer the dolphins would remain with them. Divers who swam towards the dolphins, or attempted to grab them, were left alone.

Human fear seemed to be an important factor in cases where dolphin approaches to people had been very brief. I suspect the divers thought they were meeting a shark or were uncertain about sharing the ocean with something bigger than themselves. Then our newsletters began to present dozens of satisfactory accounts.

From the outset we were most anxious to encourage an ethical code for inter-species encounters. All the finest experiences on our file showed that people should not impose themselves on dolphins—they will gain very little. High-quality episodes occur spontaneously. The dolphins make the choice. If the humans are unafraid, the encounter may intensify. But if dolphins, orca or whales are chased, encircled or buzzed by outboards, they will simply withdraw. Our initial newsletters state this explicitly:

Playing with Dolphins

'It is difficult to say which ingredients in our set-up are essential, but we have had many successful, prolonged interlocks. Most people find that while dolphins bow-ride, they leave if you get in with them. They may be frightened or holding out to establish equable human/dolphin rules.

'We feel it is vital to avoid any tendency towards manipulating dolphins to our own ends. We must not harass them, encircle them, or in any way force our presence on them. Remember the Marine Mammals Protection Act. Even using a camera should be done with discretion—it can spoil the spontaneity of interlock. A receptive mood is best for all on board. It is better to leave cameras out of it for a while or they'll find you dull—it's hard to be playful and spontaneous with a headful of 'f' stops.

'When we sight dolphins now we just heave to or beat quietly about in their vicinity. From our forward beam hangs a bell that we ring about six times when they surface for air. This establishes our acoustic identity. If they are not too busy herding fish, they will leap out and head over to us. We play carefully chosen music through our bows, especially flute and wind instruments. This tunes us in to their presence.

'When they come on our bows we play a special "message tape" that would take a lot of space to explain but only seconds to demonstrate. It is an analogue statement about the low-frequency sound channels we and the great whales use and the high frequencies used by dolphins. Meanwhile, we are on the bows or in the nets enjoying being with them.

'Mutual trust can be established as long as we place ourselves within access of the dolphins—so that each species is equally vulnerable to the other. It seems wrong to us to try to touch the dolphins—a sudden lunge may succeed, but that is a kind of rape and startles the creatures. The interlock approach is to hold out your hand—show them a human limb, its joints and expressiveness, demonstrating this unusual limb to a friendly alien. The dolphins may examine it, swimming on their sides, and eventually one may approach and nudge your hand.

'With powerboats, bow-riding is potentially very dangerous and a safety harness may be necessary. That's why we prefer sail and we know they're not attracted merely by engine noise.

'We find when we meet a group of dolphins there are usually certain individuals that are most attentive and keep returning again and again. It is important to observe any with distinctive fin markings—you may then be able to recognise this group when you meet again and a body of shared experience will develop: friendship. A telephoto lens with high-speed film is very good to record any distinctive fin markings. We have a cardboard dorsal fin as a template on the outline of which we record distinctive markings, with the date and location.

'Once mutual trust has been established, you can slow the boat right down, while one diver at a time leaps in and engages their interest by dolphin-diving down. Meanwhile, the boat circles back and stops. If you are all frolicsome enough the dolphins may stay—even teach you tricks.

'Don't be disappointed if interlock is not successful. Dolphins may have a variety of reasons for not playing—an important fish-herding manoeuvre may be in progress—like cowboys on the big roundup. There is considerable evidence that dolphins may sense if there is somebody on board who does not want to be involved with them and would prefer to be fishing—or actually fears them. So if it doesn't happen, leave it for another day. In some cases the dolphins may return later in a playful mood, when work is over for the day.

'We feel it is essential to extend to dolphins the same courtesies and thoughtfulness as when visiting people in a strange village. Remember that man is inherently boring to these ocean nomads—many of the things we do are to heighten interest in us. The message tape, the rondels, and the dolphin suit we wear may not be essential, but our system appears to work. When you enter the water it is important to avoid swimming straight at them. Treat them like villagers on a strange island, or oceanic nomads who may have a low opinion of human intelligence but are curious to explore our behaviour and our capacity for joy, if we meet them in a humble and creative manner.

'With snorkelling gear, start diving down, always doing the dolphin-swim, or kick and stay below as much as possible. They start to mimic us, and seemingly lampoon our attempts to mimic them! This is the beginning of body-language communication, just as between mother and child or people from alien cultures. So far the dolphins have responded in a variety of surprising ways, which suggest that this line of research, if carried out more extensively, would produce some very interesting insights into the nature of their social patterns and the purpose of their large brains, quite beyond what can be learnt from individuals in captivity.

'On three occasions while wearing her dolphin suit, Jan has had individual dolphins bond with her, like friendly puppies not wanting to leave her side, seemingly indicating she should swim off with them. We have had *Delphinus* play with us for up to 4 hours 20 minutes, and in each case it has been our side that had to break it off from sheer exhaustion.

'From these games-play sessions we are learning constantly and we keep modifying our approach flexibly in the light of new findings. We have learnt to identify individuals from their fin patterns and often know when we are meeting old friends.'

INTERLOCK QUESTIONNAIRE

Sea & weather conditions: ....
Date & time of day: ....
Boat name: ....
Position: ....
How did boat/dolphins first approach? ....
How did dolphins behave *before* you
   got in? ....
Number of divers in water? ....
Number with scuba? ....
Person first in? ....
Dolphin species? ....
Approximate number of dolphins? ....
Any with peculiar markings? ....
Were there any young present? ....
How small? ....
Any surface or underwater shots showing
   recognisable fins? ....
What do you think held their interest so
   long? ....
How many cameras in water? ....
Owners' names & addresses: ....
Any unusual items of dolphin behaviour, such as:
   —tail-first sinking? ....
   —jaws opening & closing? ....
   —seaweed trailing from fins, jaws, etc.? ....
   —bubbles gushing from blowhole? ....
   —defecating as a possible signal (i.e., close
   to a diver & right in his field of vision)? ....
How did the divers behave, such as:
   —snorkelling down frequently? ....
   —swimming coordinately in pairs, etc.? ....
   —forward rolls? ....
How close did they approach divers at
   any time? ....
How did interlock terminate: did divers
   or dolphins withdraw first? ....
Approximate duration of interlock? ....
Any special remarks ....

Please add your name & address and send this report to:
Project Interlock HQ, PO Box 20, Whangarei, New Zealand

Tour of New Zealand Dolphin Swimming Locations

Feedback from our newsletters came from one end of New Zealand to the other: Spirits Bay to Foveaux Strait. Naturally there was a bias towards those areas where diving is intensive all year around and where dolphins developed an early rapport with humans, such as the Poor Knights Islands. But generally these anecdotes provide an excellent guide to some of the best dolphin swimming locations in the world. And, rather than trying to distil for the reader the essence of how to engage the interest of dolphins and explore their creativity, I can offer nothing better than the accumulated play experience of so many people. Once you absorb this, an intuitive process develops: you just know how to improvise, as the situation unfolds. As you read this assemblage, I hope you will have the same thrill Jan and I experienced as we saw certain patterns emerge in the range of dolphin responses to humans—patterns that offer insights and glimmerings of understanding: why do these sea creatures show such interest in humans? How should we behave in encountering them? What is the human potential for communicating with them? What messages are they sending out to us? Please draw your own conclusions from all the evidence here.

Besides providing a geography of potential dolphin encounters, this is also a history of their unique development in New Zealand—in each area I have followed a time-line. This means that, in some cases, initial accounts, often tinged with fear, may be quite modest, even a little dull. But I feel that such a context is really necessary in order to appreciate the white-hot excitement of those episodes where the dolphin swimmers really got it right. Most of all, I hope, if you learn something new during an encounter, you will give Project Interlock* further feedback.

* PO Box 20, Whangarei—please send a stamped envelope for reply.

9: Far North Dolphin Encounters

The northernmost dolphin encounter in our file comes from Spirits Bay, where Jaan Voot and Jeff Pearch were searching a rather barren wave-swept reef for crays. (Encounters at the Kermadecs and Three Kings Islands have been reported, but nothing intensive.)

Spirits Bay, February 1979, Jaan: 'Getting to the end of the dive, we were about 15 metres down when Jeff tapped my shoulder and we saw a pair of dolphins disappearing into the misty murk on the edge of visibility. I gave a call like 'Yahoo' into my regulator. Within seconds the same dolphins, or another pair, approached us again from another direction. This time they came in close.

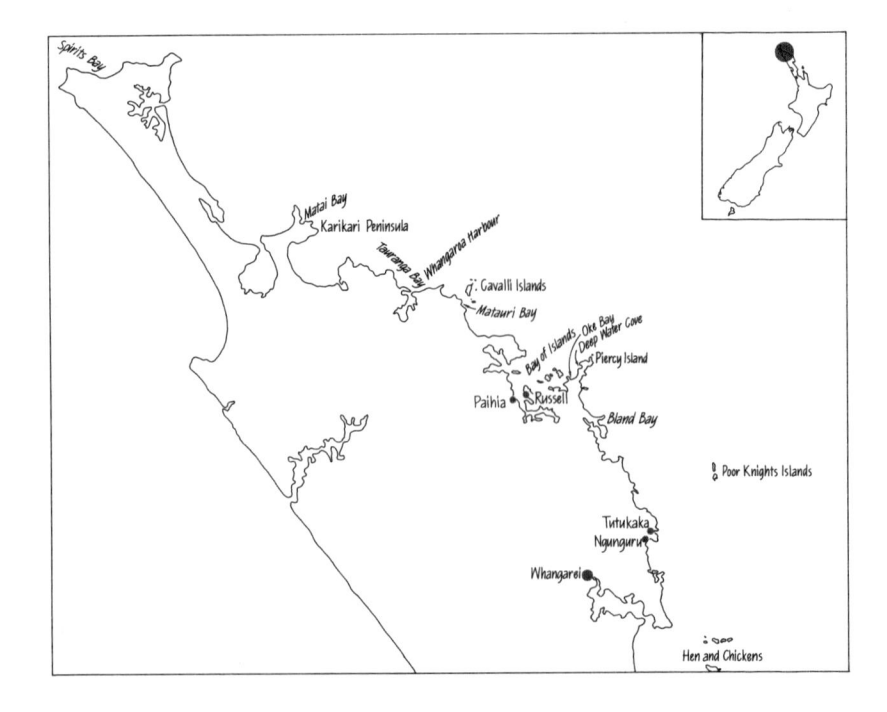

'I had never appreciated how mammalian bottlenose dolphins were: when they were approaching us, head on, they were turning their heads sideways to look at us. I knew that the head and neck allow movement up and down, but I didn't realise that they could turn their heads to each side to give each eye a chance to look.

'Again I was standing and shouting 'Yahoo' as they circled us close. The two dolphins swam with exactly the same movement—as if both tail strokes were controlled by the same brain. They kept close formation even as they circled, turned and circled. Maybe we were very insignificant to them, and when their curiosity had been satisfied they glided off into the blue.'

Matauri Bay, 4 March 1979

Down at Matauri Bay, a few weeks later, Dave Stallworthy noticed five bottlenose playing, so decided to launch a boat. When they came very close to it, he leapt in with his camera.

'They repeatedly swam close, but I had difficulty in taking good photographs as they swam very fast and always approached from behind me. The vest I was wearing was so tight it was affecting my snorkelling.

'Two of the dolphins always appeared to swim together. One dolphin appeared friendlier (or braver?) than the others. I repeatedly duck dived, dolphin-kicking, and generally tried to amuse the dolphins.

'After about half an hour they were gradually keeping further away, or sweeping in less frequently, and I was getting tired, and I think I had also finished the film.

'Evidently they stayed in the bay for two or three hours, and often one or another would leap from the water.'

Matai Bay

On New Years Day 1982 at the end of Karikari Peninsula, while swimming at beautiful Matai Bay, David Campbell sighted dolphins offshore.

'The group of about 30 bottlenose dolphins came closer in to the beach and we could see that they were feeding. A friend and I ran and got our snorkelling gear, no wetsuits, and entered from the beach. By this time the dolphins were heading back out to sea. Two people in a canoe were following. We had to swim a long way out into very deep water before we caught up and had to continue swimming to keep up with them. We never did get closer than 20 metres from the main group. Small groups of about five or ten dolphins would detach from the feeding mob to come and investigate us.

'When the first individuals appeared I was immediately impressed by their size. I think it was significant that a small group would come around us, leave, then another would come around. At first the dolphins stayed at the limit of visibility, about 6 metres, but they soon came within a metre. We dived down to follow them as they swam below us, and they generally led us around in circles, just keeping out of arm's reach. Once, as I dived down, one dolphin passed very close behind me and bowled me slightly with its wake. Once a mother and baby dolphin came around. I did two circuits with them, 4 metres down.

'I was most struck by the way they would closely examine you with their eyes, and one animal opened its mouth as it went by. The water was full of bits of whatever they were feeding on. Someone told me that they often defecate as a friendly gesture.

'We decided we were getting too far from shore so concluded our encounter and began to swim for the beach. The whole encounter lasted for about ten minutes.'

Cavalli Islands

A few weeks later Brian McMurray and his diving friends were returning to Matauri Bay after diving at the Cavalli Islands.

'As we came past the large bay on the land side of the biggest island, we noticed two small power boats and a motor sailer close by a school of dolphins. After several minutes watching we put on our snorkelling gear and joined the others already playing in the water with the dolphins.

'The dolphins, bottlenose, were quite large, approximately 3 metres, and several of them had juveniles with them about 80 centimetres to 1 metre in length.

'Although the dolphins remained just out of reach, they would come swimming up and pass our bodies within centimetres and leap out of the water. If we dived down about 3 metres they would flash past, turning over to watch us. Several of the older dolphins were throwing fish in the air and catching them again; it was almost as if someone had been teaching them tricks. They were extremely playful and would swim between our legs, but as much as we tried to catch hold of the dorsal fin and get a ride we couldn't: they were just too fast and agile.

'I noticed as soon as a swimmer got between an adult and a juvenile, the adult would quickly move back to the side of the juvenile again. Each time I went to the surface and purged my snorkel, dolphins would appear quickly around me. I tested this several times when there were no dolphins in sight and it worked each time. The school was moving around the bay. I think they were reasonably easy to keep up with, although we got towed behind my boat on a float a couple of times.

'After we had been in the water about half an hour we got back into the boat and did a count. There were between 20 and 30 dolphins around then, including the young ones.'

In June the following year, 1993, Jacqui and Dover Samuels were heading out to the largest of the Cavalli Islands from their home in Matauri Bay, to catch piper.

'As we motored into Wai-iti Bay, there in front of us, to our great excitement, was a school of approximately 20 bottlenose dolphins; it was obvious that they had not long eaten and were in a relaxed and playful mood. None showed any signs of fear or anxiety at our presence, and in fact a number were eager to ride the bow wave of the boat.

'The group's swimming pattern was evident: usually about ten mothers with calves congregated together. Another four stayed close, about 10 metres away, and the rest in twos and threes were lolling around, sometimes 50 to a 100 metres away from the main gatherings, yet each couple staying close together.

'Dover and I decided to dash home to collect masks, flippers and the underwater camera. On our return the school had moved south and were around Tarawera Island; they were still unagitated and the formation could only be described as an unruly circle, but the same clusters still existed. I manned the boat and Dover was in the water in seconds. At first they appeared a little wary but certainly not frightened, keeping their distance and slowly moving around the channel. Shortly afterwards it was my turn.

'This was my first chance to meet dolphins in the water. Dover, on the other hand, had swum with dolphins before.

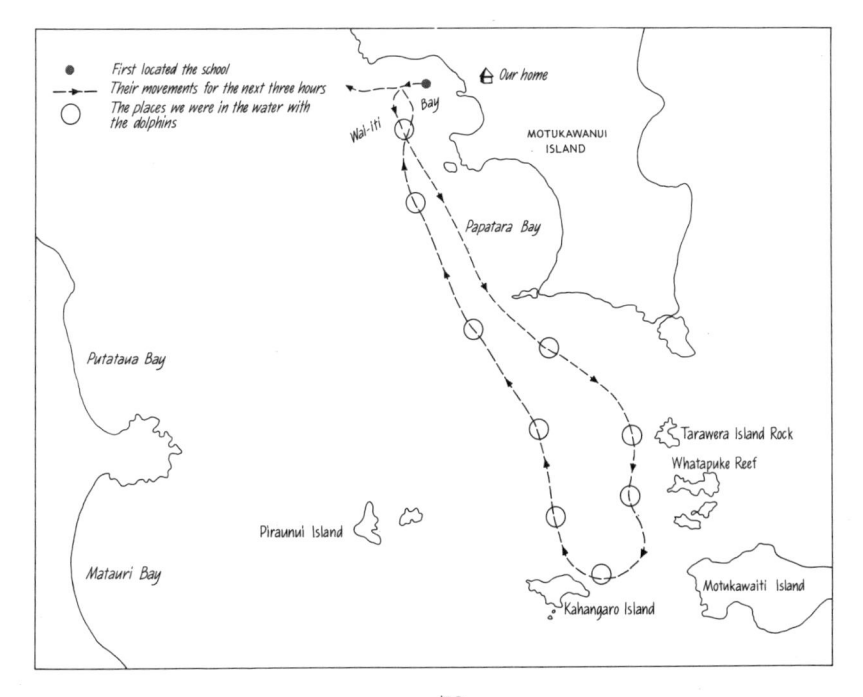

'I was not in the slightest bit hesitant or fearful; in fact I felt nothing but excitement and exhilaration. I could see a couple in the distance, but they were not close enough to take a photo. As they began to move towards the shallower water, between Motukawaiti and Kahangaro Islands, I returned to the boat and we followed them. Visibility was about 30 metres; and the bottom, around 20 metres at its deepest part, could clearly be seen. For the next three hours, Dover and I took turns, in and out of the water, with these magnificent creatures. The different personalities of individuals were evident: some were wary and kept a reasonable distance, some friendly and playful, and others quite boisterous—they could easily be described as the showoffs. We would both try to imitate their movements, and often individuals would deliberately copy us. They became very playful, rolling on their backs, slapping the water with their tails; tail-standing, and of course making acrobatic leaps into the air. The water was alive with their high-pitched chatter, easily heard even if the dolphins were out of sight.

'During my time with them in the water, the main group would often swim directly under me half on their sides, peering at me. They all seemed very curious: some would swim around me, crisscrossing in front, and others would swim towards me gently, veering to the right or left a metre away. The majority were quite large, around 2.5–3.5 metres in length. Under the water up close, they looked even longer. One particular dolphin swam within arm's length having a good look at this person trying to imitate him. I was attempting to roll from side to side in a dolphin-like manner, and as he swam in front of me, he quite obviously copied me, rolling his body from one side to another, then swam off. I was thrilled, to say the least. He wasn't going to let me touch him, but to me that incident was the next best thing.

'Dover had the camera each time he was in the water, and managed to shoot two rolls of film. I must admit he can certainly imitate the dolphin much better than I, and two large dolphins that seemed to take up the rear of the school became quite friendly towards him, darting around him, while another caught a marblefish and was having fun tossing it in the air, and then decided to tease Dover under the water, with the same fish. A couple, presumably a male and female, were on the bottom, one lying on its back and the other over its mate's stomach. Whether they were mating or just playing, we are not sure.

'Each time we followed them in the boat, they took great joy in riding the bow wave and leaping out of the water, while I was madly leaning over the side of the boat, tapping the bow with my hand. At times they were so close—a few more centimetres and I could have touched them.

'By the time the three hours had elapsed, the school had completed a circle and ended up back in Wai-iti Bay, still in no hurry to move out to sea, just frolicking on the surface. Dover was back in the water with them for the last time. They darted around him, one swimming between his legs. They had certainly overcome any shyness they had experienced when we first entered the water.

'Unfortunately, Dover and I were cold and physically tired, after three hours of trying to keep up with their movements and games, so we left our school of incredible cetaceans and headed home. At 10.45 the next morning I watched, through a pair of binoculars, another small group of about six, heading south through the channel; however this group was on the move.'

Whangaroa Area

In April the following year, 1984, Dave Stephens was diving in the same area, slightly to the north, when he met a dozen bottlenose.

'It was a sunny day with an incoming tide, and the school was moving eastward towards Wainui Bay, quite slowly but faster than I could swim.

'The dolphins did not really stop at any point and play, but they did interact with people. We would get in front of them and enter the water as they came by.

'On several occasions dolphins defecated in the water in front of us with almost constant whistling. Generally they would turn on their side and watch us as they passed. Once a large adult turned back and from a range of about 2 metres examined me. I could feel the clicks almost coming from inside my head. I'm not sure I liked it much. I was very much the junior partner in this part of the interlock. None of the others were examined in this way, but they were generally just watching from the surface. I tried to dive to dolphin level and dolphin-kick like mad.

'The dolphin that gave me the once-over had a funny fin and mark to the right-hand side of its back. Another had a notch out of the back of the fin. We broke off our contact first.'

Whangaroa, 12 February 1985

In February, a year later, John Crossman met a small group of dolphins in a shallow rocky inlet on the landward side of Arrow Rocks. (Near Tauranga Bay, this is only a short distance from the Cavallis.) There were many rocks just breaking the surface, and the dolphins seemed to be rubbing and sliding over and between the weed-festooned rocks.

'Visibility in the inlet was not good, and the activity of the group in such shallow and confined water had stirred things up.

'The group acknowledged my presence by each making a pass and having a look at me, but there was insufficient depth or space between boulders to allow the free movement for comfortable contact either way.

'The group later left the inlet and departed for the beach on the mainland with much high leaping and somersaulting.

'We moved out to the seaward side of the island where, about 20 minutes later, the group reappeared. Initially their interest centred on tearing in and out of the white water over the reef and once again sliding and rubbing over the exposed rocks.

'I re-entered the water (now 11 metres deep and with good visibility) and began performing just below the surface. Within seconds their clicking and whistling announced their approach and they circled, investigating me for 20 minutes or so until I had had about as much as I could physically take. I returned to the boat, and they went back to the white water along the edge of the island.

'As it was our intention originally to go fishing, we completed our circuit of the island and headed out to a small reef that breaks about 800 metres offshore. Before the little 25-horsepower Johnson had pushed us half the distance, however, the largest and most assertive of the group rejoined the boat, swimming alongside and looking up at the three of us. My two companions included Paul, a 15-year-old, and his father.

'So, in again—this time I persuaded Paul to come in too, for a once-in-a-lifetime experience. Somewhat reluctantly, clad only in togs, mask and snorkel, he followed me in and remained on the surface.

'The whole group immediately returned, five mature and two juveniles. The "leader", the largest and most assertive, had two nicks out of its dorsal. The "second in command" also had a nick and a very worn trailing edge on its tail! The assertive two-nick dolphin was trailing a piece of weed over the leading edge of its tail. It was not in any way attached or tangled, just draped once over the leading edge. I don't know how it managed to keep it in place, but the weed was obvious, right up until we returned to the boat, despite its antics.

'The group viewed Paul from below but made no attempt at close passes, perhaps sensing his apprehension. However, they kept approaching me, 5 metres down, in twos and threes, very close but not within touching distance. My lasting impression of this contact was of beaks approaching unexpectedly—particularly from behind, while my attention was focused on other members in front.

'The group defecated frequently on this last contact, and we were accompanied by a school of small snapper, the closest we got to fishing all day! Snapper feed on their faeces.

'We finally withdrew, Paul because of the cold and me from exhaustion. The dolphins remained in the area until we parted.'

Footnote: On 14 February 1984, our catamaran, RV *Interlock*, met an aggregation of longfin pilot whales, *Globicephala melaena*, and bottlenose dolphins near Whangaroa in the far north. From their behaviour we think they were feeding co-operatively on squid. While they were close around our vessel, we recorded their noisy whistling and click chains. Then we played synthesised click chains up and down the scale, through our sound array, listening for any responses. To our utter incredulity, Jan and I heard and recorded perfect runs up the scale, exactly mimicking our output. We do not know whether this was whale or dolphin. It does indicate that echolocation clicks, besides their role in prey location and navigation, can be adapted to playful or communicative ends.

Bay of Islands

Further south, at the Bay of Islands, another series of encounters began in January 1981. The dolphins involved could quite easily be the same pod as at the Cavallis, 60 kilometres away, but more than one group of dolphins include the Bay of Islands in their range.

For Dave Ellery this was his first encounter: 'We caught up to a large school of dolphins while on our way to a diving spot. They were headed east between Moturua Island and Tokatokahao Point in the Rawhiti Inlet. Steve and myself were half suited up, so my other mate stopped the boat and we were in the water in seconds. The dolphins at the rear of the school turned around to see what we were about. Four or five of them came up to us really close.

'I dived just under the surface to meet two dolphins heading straight for me. One was pretty large compared to the other. They swam in circles for a few moments and then disappeared. Suddenly the same two came straight for me from behind. I tried the dolphin-kick to see what their response was, but they kept on going as the rest of the school was heading away from us.

'Back on board my other mate had watched it all and said that dolphins had been going around in circles above us, and some had been leaping out of the water just in front of us. Even though it was a short encounter, we reckon we'll never forget it.'

That same month MAF diver Dave Collins was at Deep Water Cove in the Bay of Islands with two companions. It was his turn to look after the boat while they went down on scuba.

'Steve and Davy are in the final stages of getting geared up when there's a commotion of dolphin frolicking and leaping in the bay. The boys finish in double-quick time and in the dinghy, we head for the nearest dolphins. They meet us half way, and Davy and Steve are in with tanks on. The dolphins can be heard squeaking continually from the dinghy. They are a marvellous sight as they circle, bank and descend around the divers. There's surging and considerable frothing on the surface where four or five dolphins seem very excited about something, followed by three of them leaping vertically about 5 to 6 metres out of the water and splashing back down. Their bellies show pinkish when they emerge. It might not be wise for divers to get mixed up in that frolic.

'There's an estimated 15 dolphins in the cove and they seem to merge and separate in different groups of sometimes six, three, two, four, and so on. Some go right into the water's edge among the rocks, and others are out deeper. Anchovies scatter like driven spray from some, while others are leaping. The divers receive constant attention from different groups. Steve surfaces and proposes that I use his face mask and snorkel. I strip to nothing and swim in. Now I can hear clicks, as well as squeaks, and the dolphins appear immediately below. Visibility must be 11 metres, and I can see Davy sitting on the bottom away to my left. The two dolphins approach me rapidly, and just as rapidly any apprehension I had disappears. The dolphins circle, and I execute my first naked duck dive. The dolphins parade past and around, to give me the once-over.

'They're in pairs, triples and singles in beautiful formation. I dive down and I get the feeling two want me to join them in a circular movement. I try. They click. Again and again I surface and dive, and each time they try to have me co-ordinate the movement with them—to the right, down and around; the more I try, the less time I spend with them, and they probably give up in disgust.

'I'm resting on the surface when a single dolphin approaches rapidly head on. I dive towards it on impulse and am very surprised that the dolphin does the same thing. We don't collide, because the dolphin glides effortlessly underneath me. I'm back on the surface looking into the depths when a dolphin slows and I swear it moves its head up and down looking at me—once, twice, three times—emitting clicks madly. I have the positive feeling that I've been fully computerised within a second of time. I dive down. The dolphin follows and wants me to swim around in a circle—to the right again. I think the dolphin is lovely and feel the dolphin has adopted me. We play for a long time.

'Whenever the dolphin disappears, I take the snorkel out of my mouth and try to imitate dolphin squeaks under the water. The dolphin returns often with one or two others. Eventually I become cold and climb back into the dinghy, feeling relaxed and happy.

'On reflection, I must admit that some of my actions while playing with the dolphins may have been influenced by them entirely. It wasn't my idea to play with them. I only wanted to look.'

It was winter time, a few months later, when Jeff Couchman met a group of about seven bottlenose near Oke Bay, in the Bay of Islands. All large adults, they were fossicking around rocks in the shallows.

'They made the customary slow passes at me—to within about 2 metres, for about ten minutes, and then continued on their coastal swim, again right against the shoreline. I was then surprised to see one them repeatedly lunging half out of the water and flicking seaweed into the air, as if playing. At the time I was about 20 metres away and saw it flicking the weed five to six times.*

'On the habit of fossicking around rocks, I recall having seen bottlenose doing exactly the same at the Cavallis many years ago. They were fossicking in the sand at a rock/sand interface.'

It was midwinter a year later when Jeff Couchman met four bottlenose adults outside Cathedral Cave, Piercy Island, at the southern entrance to the Bay of Islands. They were swimming amid schoolfish, when he leapt in alone.

'I was confronted by the four, closely grouped and on or just under the surface, making their initial head-on pass. I swam with them for about 15 minutes, during which time they would come directly at me, just under the surface, pass very close, and then dive straight down under me to 11 metres, disappearing briefly before repeating the performance. Fortunately I had a still camera with me and got some quite good shots despite fairly dirty water—10 metres visibility.

'Two weeks later I again saw a group of four bottlenose, this time at the Cavallis. I was spearfishing with a friend at Bait Rock (on the northeastern side of the main island). We were hunting kingfish in 30 metres of water, with visibility of 30 metres, with masses of schoolfish feeding in the area—kahawhai, trevally, koheru, and pink maomao—when the bottlenose turned up. They approached on the surface with the kahawhai fleeing in front of them, but came no closer than 6 metres. I am convinced that they know what spearguns are all about. They stayed in the area for over an hour, making numerous passes around us to check us over during that time. They were definitely feeding, as from time to time the packed kahawhai would suddenly stop feeding on krill, pack into a solid mass, and race off into the blue. Shortly after the dolphins would appear to give us the once-over again. Their behaviour was very interesting: after I'd speared my kingie, they would approach very slowly to close range, obviously knowing the gun had been discharged, and almost hover while looking at me, then go straight down to the struggling kingie and swim around with it for a while.

* Around this time we received three reports of bottlenose dolphins playing seaweed games. In the Poor Knights area, near Trevor's Rock, some were seen rolling in seaweed, and one approached a photographer with a piece draped around its dorsal. In South Harbour Dave Probert saw dolphins flick seaweed into the air, leap and land on top of it. Near the Hen and Chickens he saw about 12 bottlenose playing with a ball of seaweed so skilfully it was never allowed to touch the water.

'We gave up spearing after an hour or so as the schoolfish were getting very nervous—what with divers and dolphins having a go at them at the same time—and swapped guns for camera.

'Later in the day the dolphins moved towards the northern tip of the Cavallis and when last seen were swimming around a commercial fishing boat.

'From what I have been told by another group of divers, who saw a similar group of dolphins while spearfishing in the same area three weeks before our trip, it seems likely that the bottlenose stayed in the area for a month or so.

'Undoubtedly their presence coincided with unusually good concentrations of bait fish, which were excellent all month and at a peak the day we were there—just one day before heavy storms. We returned to the Cavallis last weekend, a week after the gales, to find the area completely barren of fish and dolphins.'

In mid-March, 1985, Simon Brown's yacht *Windshadow* was anchored at Deep Water Cove when the *Tiger Lily* ferry arrived, dolphins on her bow.

'We up-anchored and motored over as the ferry left. A school of about a dozen large bottlenose dolphins approached and dived around the bows. I stopped the motor and Moira dived in. The dolphins stayed around the boat for about ten minutes before slowly moving away. The boat was drifting rapidly downwind. Moira came aboard, and I started the motor and headed in their direction. Once under way, they immediately rejoined us. This time I dived in, the boat drifting again, and counted about a dozen 'full-grown' dolphins and one about half size. They all came round, no closer than about 3 metres, and checked me out. When I started doing 'dolphin-kick' among them, they seemed to really appreciate my efforts, coming within a metre, being much more vigorous, and their squeals were far more frequent and intense. After about ten minutes I swam back to the boat, which had drifted off, one dolphin accompanying me back.

'We motored back towards them and they came over again. This time Moira played her flute from the bow, and they stayed there hardly moving, the boat just drifting. While the flute was being played, one dolphin leapt out of the water in front of the bows, coming towards us, followed by two others doing the same together. Another dolphin on the outer edge of the group slapped the water with its tail four or five times.

'They all disappeared and resurfaced a short way off two minutes later. They then came back again, so Moira jumped in, but they did not stay long this time. Moira said one dolphin had what looked like a piece of seaweed around its tail. I saw only one with a distinctive dorsal fin.'

RV *Interlock* is a James Wharram-designed Polynesian catamaran equipped for meeting dolphins. The bow hammocks offer easy water access, and the bows transmit stereo sound. (Photo: Wade Doak)

Jan Doak mimics dolphin body language. (Photo: Wade Doak)

Interlock begins with bottlenose dolphins, *Tursiops truncatus,* leaping as rhythmic music is transmitted underwater from RV *Interlock*'s special sound system. (Photo: Barry Fenn)

Eventually mothers and babies come close. This tiny dolphin is being 'nursed' by two adults. Dolphin babies feed every 15 minutes, day and night. (Photo: Wade Doak)

Among the dolphins on Nudelock Day were a number of individuals from previous meetings who seemed to signal us when we were slow to recognise them. At the outset a certain dolphin came very close, hovering between our bows where Tony Ayling skimmed the surface in the hammock, his camera just beneath. Nicks in the dorsal fin and the figure-eight pattern on its side enabled us to recognise it: Simo. (Photo: Dr Tony Ayling)

After a lunch break we met what we thought was a second group of dolphins. But our pictures told us otherwise: Simo was there, trying to attract our attention. While his usual companion defecates right in front of the lens, Simo trails seaweed around his tail, his fins, his jaw . . . Simo, we were to learn, has quite a history of friendly approaches to people, brandishing bits of seaweed. (Photo: Wade Doak)

Bay of Islands dolphin swimming with bottlenose dolphins. (Photo: Jo Berghan, Dolphin Encounters, Paihia)

Alf Millar of Te Ngaere Bay, Northland, meets a huge bottlenose that came into his arms while bathing. (Photo: Deke Millar)

Dolphin swimming in Mercury Bay: meeting common dolphins. (Photos, from top: Rod Rae, Rod Rae, Vivienne Wood, Mercury Bay Seafaris)

Swimming with the dusky dolphins of Kaikoura. (Photos: Brent McFadden, New Zealand Sea Adventures)

Swimming with the dusky dolphins of Kaikoura. (Photos: Dennis Buurman, Dolphin Encounters)

Swimming with the Hector's dolphins of Catlins Bay, Southland. (Photos: Donna MacIntosh, Koramika Charters, Invercargill)

10: Dolphin Encounters in the Poor Knights Area

In the Poor Knights area, following our own intensive series of encounters, divers continue to meet bottlenose dolphin pods that seem to include these islands in their range, especially during winter months, but quite often in January too. Common dolphins are met more frequently during springtime.

Because this area is one of the most popular diving areas in New Zealand, and perhaps because of our own input, the frequency and complexity of encounters are of a high order. We think dolphins in this region have developed a readiness to interact with divers, which will be apparent from these accounts.

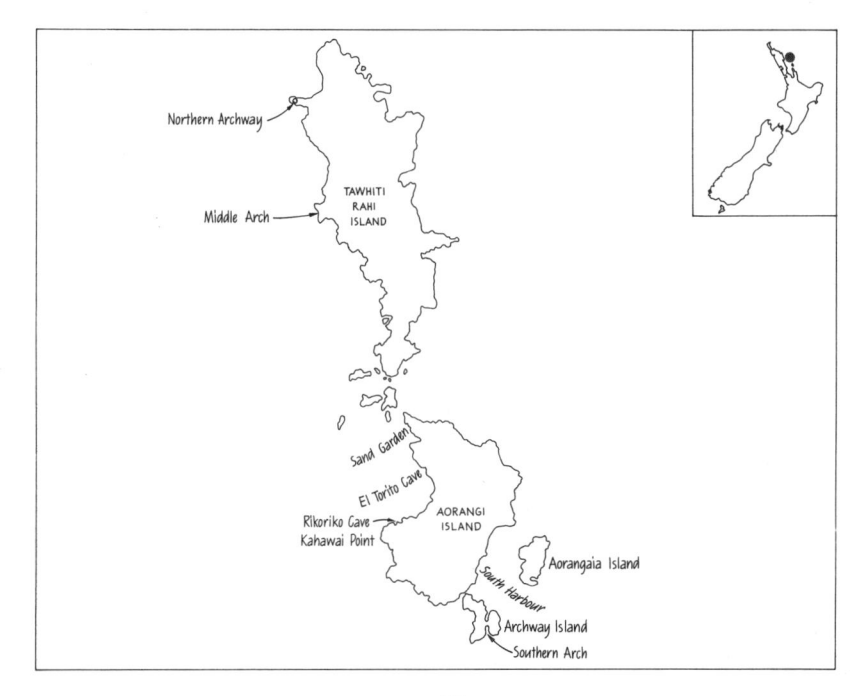

Graham Thomson was diving in the Poor Knights area in mid-winter 1978 and met a group of bottlenose dolphins with whom we have had contact on a number of occasions. As other divers approached these dolphins in a similar friendly manner, they too found the dolphins most responsive to playful antics and mimicry.

On 13 June 1978 Graham was aboard *Lady Jess*, nearing the Pinnacles, when some 200 bottlenose approached and several began bow-riding.

The vessel anchored, and 15 divers, only two with scuba, including Graham, entered the water. Some began doing the dolphin-kick, snorkelling down frequently with fancy manoeuvres and forward rolls. Some of the dolphins remained with them for about 40 minutes. There were young present, about six to eight, in the group that stayed.

Graham remarks: 'The dolphin in my photo (one which Jan and I had met frequently) was by far the most playful and seemed to be the instigator in evolving the games we attempted to play. The others played and observed us, but he was the most interested. He would come straight towards us at breakneck speed and stop instantaneously about a metre away, then spin round and round us two or three times before zooming in again. We saw the jaw-open-and-closing gesture.

'If we did the dolphin-kick, at least two or three dolphins, sometimes more, would swim parallel with us. We tried doing forward and backward rolls. My camera housing made this difficult. My buddy, Andy Smyth, managed some strange antics that attracted a fair bit of attention. Andy proved the sort of guy you want when playing with dolphins. He seemed to know when to sit back and watch and when to play.

'Mothers were bringing their young in fairly close, to within a metre, and the young were on the inside towards us, as if Mum was saying to them, 'Go on, have a good look. They're too clumsy to hurt you.'

'This sort of thing lasted around 40 minutes until we were exhausted and had to retire to the boat.

'On board we could see they had broken up into separate groups—some with each pair of divers. People wearing scuba couldn't get anywhere near as close as those just on snorkel.

'The dolphins hung around for most of the day while we had towed scuba-dives, joining a number of us when down on scuba.

'There was no real topside action, fancy leaps, etc. other than coming up and checking on the boat when it was moving around picking up divers. It was interesting to see the number of snapper feeding below the dolphins.'

In late February the following year, 1979, Graham Thomson and his friends met bottlenose on the coast about 50 kilometres from the Poor Knights.

'On the shore side of Danger Rock in the entrance to Bland Bay we came across a school of bottlenose dolphins on two separate days. On the first, we spent over an hour in their company. We had a great time with them: barrel rolls and chasing each other. One of them, easily recognisable by the pieces missing from its tail fin, was a real sport. It would have races with you. I found that by descending to 5 metres and remaining there until this particular animal drew level, then doing the dolphin-kick, it would race me until I ran out of air and then, just as I started to surface, it would speed up and pass, only to remain in the same area till I recovered for another race.

'The next day we saw them again in the same spot and had the pleasure of their company for over an hour. It could have been longer, but they, being fitter, outlasted us easily. We performed basically the same manoeuvres and games as the day before and had lots of fun. The guys on the trip who had never been with dolphins before were really blowing their minds.

'I tried getting towed behind the boat. I had 50 metres of rope out and was hanging onto a buoy at the end. It took a while, but eventually they came and swam right next to me, and together we performed barrel rolls at a slightly higher speed than I could attain on my own. Up until this point they had been quite active on top of the water, but the moment I hopped in all topside activity ceased. I was told this by the people in the boat. During this time they never got as close as before: about a metre was the limit.

'I eventually got tired and couldn't stand the pace, so I pulled myself back onto the boat. About 30 seconds later a group of about eight dolphins charged the stern of the boat and less than 2 metres from where I was sitting four leapt into the air in unison. I could have reached out and touched them. As they plunged in right next to me, all the boys on the boat clapped in response to the show. From then on the dolphins played among themselves, performing leaps in the air. As many as three or four would be in the air at once. Twice they actually touched, glancing off each other.'

It was in spring 1979 that Graham Adams set out on a dive trip to the Poor Knights on the charter vessel *Norseman*. He met two species of dolphins and whales!

'We were out of Tutukaka about an hour, when six common dolphins were spotted on the starboard side about 400 metres away from the launch. They appeared to be feeding, working in a small circle with a large number of gannets hovering above. The cool northerly whisked the smooth sea into sheets of ruffles like crushed velvet.

'After spotting the dolphins, an air of excitement was present on the launch, and this was magnified when the skipper sighted whales ahead. All we saw was the occasional spout on the horizon, but as luck would have it there were some travelling south about 100 metres from the launch. We then spotted a single whale, a straggler, coming towards us.

We changed course to have a closer look. The whale was a large black one. The sea was alive with thousands of birds; all seemed to be waiting for something to happen—gulls, mutton birds, and smaller water-hopping birds.

'We had a dive on the eastern side of the Knights, and this in itself was exciting as we hadn't dived on that coast before. We rounded the southern end of the islands and navigated through the Southern Arch: on looking across the South Harbour the water was alive with dolphins, perhaps 100 or more bottlenose cruising up and down and around the harbour. Everywhere you looked there were dolphins in twos and threes. When the dolphins heard the boat, a few played around it while others began to shoot off, leaping high out of the water.

'There was a mad scramble on board, struggling and wriggling into tight suits, fumbling with tanks and regulators, more haste less speed. Only one thing was in mind—to get into the water and play with the dolphins. By the time most of us were ready to lower ourselves into the water, the dolphins had lost interest and were moving away. The skipper, checking everyone was on board, motored off to intercept them. Then it was abandon ship, everyone into the water right in the path of sea-going travellers. We had made it in seconds and were surrounded with mystical, playful dolphins. You could hear the sonic squeaks as they communicated with each other.

'The dolphins moved quickly and effortlessly, coming straight at you and then turning or diving at the very last second. The more we played in the sea, imitating their diving, spiralling, twisting and turning, and dolphin-kicking, the more they would come close and investigate.

'The excitement lasted for 15 minutes, and then the dolphins moved on. We went back to the boat, exhausted but ecstatic.'

In spring the following year, 1980, Phillip Meyer was on the charter boat *Lady Jess*, another vessel whose skipper is enthusiastic and experienced with dolphins.

'We had been in the water about 12 minutes when I first noticed them. After recovering from amazement, I pointed them out to my buddy. We then swam, dolphin-kicking towards them. As they swam away, I started calling them through my mouthpiece: "Hey, dolphins! Come back. Come here. I love you." They were whistling, then turned away again. Some more calls through the mouthpiece and they returned for a few more minutes before finally swimming off. We were in quite shallow water close to the reef, about 10 metres.

'We regained the boat and motored around the point, where we again made contact, this time with 20 dolphins. My son Sterling Meyer, aged 12, snorkelled with them, dolphin-kicking, and Adele Lapwood, who took her camera, did too. We followed them around the bay almost to Rikoriko Cave. They ended the encounter by swimming off. There were always three or four around both swimmers and they came within a few centimetres of our reach. This episode lasted about 15 minutes.'

In December that year Grant Couchman met common dolphins in their most usual area, about 5 kilometres out from the Poor Knights where inshore and offshore currents meet and plankton animals are concentrated.

'The sea was glassy smooth, and the weather fine at around 11 a.m. About 20 dolphins were milling about in circles on the surface beneath petrels and gulls. A small sunfish was also in the area, having jumped clear of the water shortly before we sighted the dolphins. On approaching the school, six of their number surrounded our small runabout, and with the outboard stopped they proceeded to circle and have a good look at us. I grabbed fins and mask and with just a pair of baggies on entered the water, it being warm and reasonably clear, with 20 metres visibility.

'The six immediately swam in close, and when I'd snorkelled down a metre or so they swam around and under me in tight circles. After a few minutes, all but two swam off to join the main school about 30 metres away. The remaining pair continued to stay with me, at times swimming away, then quickly returning to within arm's reach. I made no attempt to touch them during the close passes. After about five minutes I returned to the boat to grab my camera and then stayed with them for another five to ten minutes before breaking off the contact to continue out to the Knights.

'Occasionally two or three dolphins, presumably from the main group, would join the pair around me and then leave as quickly as they came.

'Primarily the contact was made at or near the surface. The underwater "chit chat" from the school was constant and loud throughout the encounter. On more than one occasion, I saw an adult with a small calf. In all it was a great start to the day and a swim I'll remember for some time'.

In September 1982 a group of nine divers aboard charter boat *Norseman* had a superb bottlenose dolphin encounter at the Poor Knights, equal to those Jan and I had experienced earlier. Some of the dolphins were individuals we had met on Nudelock day. Matt Conmee had sought such a contact for three years, especially equipping himself with an electric towpedo fitted with a small scuba tank, for maximal agility in dolphin games.

'The weather was absolutely perfect and the visibility was good. We were all busy doing the things we most enjoy on such glorious days.

Some were already in the water, exploring the nearby reef on snorkel, while others were eating lunch. I was preparing the towpedo for a cruise around the reefs with the "pony" bottle attached, a miniature scuba rig that I have set up in the hope that one day I might be able to use it when meeting cetaceans.

'As all this was going on, skipper Bruce Going drew our attention to a tribe of bottlenose dolphins frolicking in the gap between the two main islands. We all expressed the hope that they would head our way, and Bruce said that, in his experience, they usually came into the Sand Garden area when they were in such a frolicsome mood.

'We watched spellbound, and sure enough, they began heading in our direction. I hurried to complete assembly of the "pony" bottle onto the towpedo. Then I leapt into the water and headed out to intercept their course, over the shallow reef and into the realm of the blue void. I sped out, dolphin-kicking behind the towpedo to get the most speed from it, all the while desperately hoping that I would not be ignored or avoided.

'Suddenly I was enveloped in a mass of swirling, undulating, blue-grey shapes, excreting faeces excitedly before me and emitting shrill whistles that reverberated through my body. Huge snapper milled about below the dolphins, darting in to feed on fresh excreta. The atmosphere was electrifying, hyperactive, exciting. I rammed the regulator into my mouth and descended to meet the dolphins on their own terms, keeping up the dolphin-kick all the while. This also reduced drag.

'Groups of three to five were swimming towards me on collision courses, in line-abreast formation, turning together at the last moment—always, it seemed, with the smallest of the group closest to me as I turned to match a parallel course. Often the smallest would be a juvenile, perhaps a metre long, and they would approach to almost arm's length, although not once did I reach out for them. It never occurred to me at the time, but in this way the dolphins could have steered me, and probably did, anywhere they desired.

'Frequently, when on a parallel course, I would do one or two barrel rolls, which is easy on the towpedo and can be quite fluid, but with no obvious effect or reaction. Alan told me afterwards that the dolphins immediately behind me were mimicking my barrel rolls, and yet I was disappointed at their seeming lack of response!

'By this time Bruce had moved the boat out into the frolicking group, and I was joined by five of the others, including Alan with his camera.

'At one stage I noticed a dolphin mouthing another 10 metres in front of me. It was an action that I would liken to puppies biting at one another's necks as they are running. It started up on top of the recipient, just behind the blowhole, and ran its teeth down the right-hand side and onto the belly. This, it seems, is the origin of some of the marks they bear—elaborate love bites perhaps.

'All too quickly I used up the air in the "pony" bottle and rushed back to the boat to discard the unwanted weight, returning to the group minutes later with just the bare towpedo. I resumed the same pattern of games-play as before, only slightly modified to allow porpoising, enhancing this action as best I could by exhaling before I breached the surface so that my total surface time was used for inhaling. I could only keep this up for a very short duration, as I soon became exhausted and had to remain at the surface for about five minutes to recuperate.

'I noticed that now the young ones were streaking away from the adults and coming very close to me on their own. At this point the games-play seemed to lose tempo, probably due to my exhaustion, and I began to look more closely at my playmates as they circled past me. One juvenile had a very distinctive and badly deformed lower jaw, curling out from under the top jaw towards the right so that the teeth around the point of the jaw were quite visible. Another juvenile had a very dark spot in the middle of its side just below the dorsal fin, although I cannot now be certain which side it was on. A large adult swam by with a lump of flesh missing from the right side of its lower jaw. It looked really bad, but there was no red flesh showing, only white. Another large one had some distinctive notches in its dorsal fin. I shall enclose sketches of these features for your files.

'The games-play had tapered right off, and I noticed that most of the other divers had left the water. The dolphins seemed to be leading me towards Rikoriko Cave as they swept and swirled around me, and I was quite happy to follow. I was by now about halfway across the bay when most of the dolphins faded to the edge of visibility, and a very large, very dark, and very scarred individual became foremost in my vision. It passed me from right to left, coming no closer than 6 metres and not altering course at all. I was struck by its apparent aura of quiet purpose, like that of a yogi or priest, and I felt compelled to follow it. It swam at a pace that I could easily match with the aid of the towpedo and led me into the quiet shallows, where I was amazed to see other dolphins down on the reef and up against the cliff wall nuzzling the *Eklonia*, like dogs rolling in the long grass, rolling on their backs and hanging with their heads down, inverted in the weed.

'My guide carried on at the same slow pace, turning and heading for the entrance to Rikoriko Cave. I dived down to meet the individuals playing in the weed, but they headed off in the same direction as my guide, and because they were much faster they disappeared into the distant blue.

'Then disaster: the towpedo stuttered and stopped—a faulty battery connection, I later discovered. The utter frustration of it! I hit it, shook it, and tried pushing it through the water, finally discarding it to leave it afloat while I dived below the surface, vocalising, to perhaps attract the attention of my playmates for a few more fleeting moments. They returned but were much more distant than before. I kept vocalising to try to hold their interest, but this lasted a very short time, and soon the surrounding blue was once again just a void. My last glimpse while in the water was of a tail fluke sliding underwater just off Kahawai Point. I turned and, collecting the towpedo, pushed it back to the boat, occasionally managing to thump it into life for a short burst.

'When I returned to the boat, the others were silent; some had gone off snorkelling close inshore. It was quite some time before I got the various impressions of the others on board. All were overwhelmed with the experience. One chap described how a dolphin had approached so close that he was able to reach out and run his hand down its side, feeling the soft texture of its skin. The non-divers in the group told us of the incredible leaping in twos and threes while the divers were in the water, the individual dolphins pulling at the divers' fins, playing tag with other divers until they were noticed, tail-slapping behind the boat, and also playing with pieces of seaweed.

'Afterwards I remembered that I should have looked for known individuals, but I'm afraid that it was all lost in the sheer excitement and joy of having the dream of three years fulfilled to the point of ecstasy that only the delirium of utter exhaustion can induce.

'We picked up anchor and started to depart for the Middle Arch, the site of our next dive. As we did so, the *Kitty Vane* appeared from the gap on the islands accompanied by yet more dolphins. Some broke away from her and came to frolic in our bow wave, finally leaving us with a parting gesture of fabulous leaping in pairs.

'Thinking back, I'm not sure why we didn't return to continue with our games. I'm sure that no-one on board would have objected. I guess we are conditioned by our society to stick to a routine, and we had planned to scuba-dive!'

Alan Morrison's Account

'After some time the bulk of the dolphins moved over towards Rikoriko Cave with Matt and his scooter. The rest of the snorkellers went back to the boat and I was left playing and taking photos of a large loner and a pair: one large and one small dolphin.

'After about 40 minutes I was starting to tire and turned back towards the boat. Twice I felt a gentle tug on my fins. Upon turning I saw nothing. When I got back to the *Norseman*, I was told that two dolphins had been right behind me, witnessed by two people, one in the water, one on the boat, and had twice pulled on one of my fins. I can only wish

I had been fitter and the water warmer. Could the tugging on my fin have been an expression of the dolphin's desire for me to remain longer with them? I like to think so. I was last in the water.

'The dolphin with the seaweed on its fin spent a lot of time rolling in the weed. It had a nick from its fin and looked very like Simo.

'Also, after reading your newsletter about how it seems snapper may feed on dolphin faeces: underneath the dolphins were some of the biggest snapper I've seen, and they were feeding on the faeces. Again, you could hear the dolphins before they became visible underwater.'

Mike Oliver's Account, from the Boat

'All the divers who could do so jumped into the water and snorkelled towards the dolphins. Soon dolphins were all round the boat, swimming with the people in the water. They were so close to the boat I could see scratches on their grey bodies and their "grinning" faces as they surfaced. I noticed one small dolphin latched onto a larger one—mother and child, I suppose—but there must have been other smaller dolphins, because I saw one leaping beside the cliffs with larger "performers". One bigger dolphin had rolled over onto its back and was hitting the water with its tail, producing large "whacks" right beneath the stern. One or two dolphins were in the seaweed fooling around; one of them was grabbing seaweed in his mouth. I got the occasional glimpse of Matt on his orange towpedo close to the dolphins. I noticed the odd lone dolphin chasing solitary divers and veering off when the divers realised they were being followed and turned around.

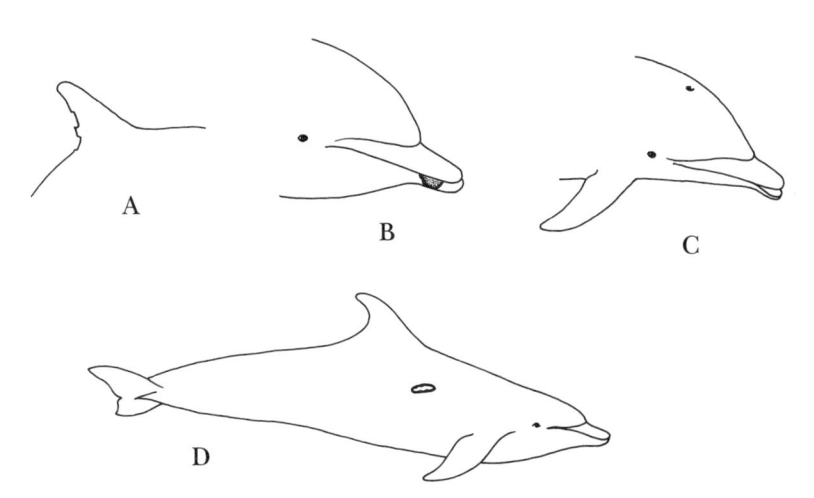

(a) Adult's fin. (b) Flesh missing from large adult's lower jaw, right side. (c) Juvenile with deformed jaw. (d) Juvenile with black mark on side.

'The little dolphin and his larger partner were into playing this "tag" game too. Eventually the dolphin group started to move towards another dive boat that had turned up, with the large lone dolphins leaving last. These seemed to remain apart from the others during most of the encounter, and two of them escorted us away from the scene, riding on or just under the bow.

'As we left for the second dive site we saw the group swimming around the other boat and divers jumping off to join them. Ahead of this boat two dolphins started leaping together and crossing over in midair as the two others had done earlier.

'Watching the dolphins and people together was an unforgettable experience, and I hope I will be lucky enough to swim as close to dolphins as my friends did. Matt summed up the whole event nicely when he said, "That made my year."'

Wade Doak's Experience

In May 1984 I was aboard *Norseman* for our annual 'geriatric divers' reunion at the Poor Knights, when I saw some curious dolphin behaviour, in much the same area as Matt Conmee. In the mid-afternoon we were heading for Red Baron Arch from the Northern Archway, when we noticed a group of dolphins near Rikoriko entrance. As they breathed on the surface, palls of vapour arose. These were bottlenose. I leapt in off El Torito Cave and saw them whirl around me—about 12, very light in colour. I moved after them until I reached the Sand Garden, where they began to frolic about. One stood on its tail, on the bottom. Another was swimming vertically with its head protruding above water. They did a series of leaps on the surface, and one spiralled in front of me.

Then I saw something quite unforgettable: a large dolphin was lying draped over a weed-covered rock in the Sand Garden, belly up, looking up at me, so I could see it was a male. Another dolphin had just left it, and another came down and nuzzled its belly from tail to head, while a third hovered alongside. The dolphins then went through the gap to the eastern side. I started to follow them, but the skipper blew the horn for me to return.

R.V. *Interlock*

On a perfect March day in 1985 the Doaks' catamaran R.V. *Interlock* was 3 kilometres off the Tutukaka coast, returning from the Poor Knights. With Wade and Jan was a young Canadian, Raphael Vigood. When bottlenose dolphins were sighted, the catamaran took a parallel course, music playing through speakers inside its bows. The dolphins turned and headed towards the boat, swarming excitedly between the bows, including one huge adult close to the starboard bow. The motor was stopped and the vessel ghosted along on a slight breeze. An underwater speaker was lowered, linked to a keyboard and a hydrophone, connected to recording gear. As soon as Wade played the first sounds through the underwater speaker, a dozen dolphins began leaping in unison. Again and again they leapt. Jan wrote in her diary:

'The air was full of excitement and we were caught up in it. Never have we had such a response before to music coming from an underwater speaker. The wind had dropped and it was flat calm. Wade said, "Get into your gear, Jan." He was already in his wetsuit but was playing underwater sound from the keyboard and at the same time had set up the recording gear to tape any sounds coming from the dolphins. In mid-ocean somebody had to mind the boat. I was trying to find my gear, carefully stowed for our trip home. I couldn't be bothered getting into my wetsuit so just grabbed my mask and snorkel and was in.

'The first dolphin I met was the very large one we had seen from the bow. It was a darker grey and it looked at me with such a wise eye. I wondered if he was a big male or the leader of the group. That was the only time I saw it, as if it had checked me out as harmless and decided it would be okay for them to stay.

'I dived, and straight away many dolphins swept in to about 3 metres, using their sonar on me. There must have been about 40 dolphins all around and under me. The water was so clear, a deep cobalt blue with almost a purple hue to it, and there was no sign of any life in the water apart from the odd jellyfish and little fluorescent dots floating by.

'Later I was stung on the arm and back by one of the tendrils from these jellyfish.

'Raphi followed me into the water. He told us later that when he first got in he could hardly get his breath. He had to gasp on the surface for a second to collect himself. He didn't know what it was—most likely excitement and the fact that this was the very first time he had ever seen dolphins in the open ocean let alone got in the water with them. I also found it difficult to hold my breath for any length of time because of the sheer excitement. It didn't matter though: I only had to be about 3 metres below the surface and the dolphins would sweep in. As time went by, they got closer and closer, so that in the end they were within touching distance. I never get the urge to touch them. I feel content just to be there with the dolphins staying close from their own choice.

'I called and made noises through my snorkel many times. The dolphins seem to be doing a lot of things that the Bahaman spotted dolphins (see *Encounters with Dolphins*, part three) had done, and as I was thinking this I saw a pair about 4 metres down mouthing each other, jaws apart, gently kissing around beak, head and down the body to the tail. It seemed to be a caress, leaving patterns of scratches from their teeth on the very delicate skins. I saw a couple belly to belly, touching pectorals. They were barrel rolling, standing vertically in the water. The mothers brought their babies in to look at us, two quite small ones. One of them left the side of its mother for a moment and then scuttled back when it realised Mother wasn't there. There were two other youngsters, and one still had the vertical birth stripes on its side.

'At first there was no defecating, but after a while one swam right in front of me and passed a long stream of faeces. After that I have never seen dolphins defecating so much, over and over again. The water was soon quite murky with it.

'The sounds in the water were amazing. I heard lots of noises in our lower frequency as well as the usual click chains and high whistles. Wade was still playing the keyboard, with long silent gaps so as to be able to hear any responses or dolphin sounds.

'The dolphins were twisting and turning in amazing patterns. Every time I dived I used the dolphin-kick. Raphi said later that he was startled by a very loud click chain series, some on the verge of pain. In fact it was so loud he thought that a dolphin must be going to brush him. Several times dolphins came up from behind us and over our shoulders, really close, whichcan be rather startling. Raphi noticed when I dived that dolphins immediately broke away from the group to come close to me.

'Wade on the boat said that it was hard to realise that they were doing that, because whenever they surfaced they were always at least 3–5 metres away from us. They most likely feel at their most vulnerable on the surface, because if anything should happen to prevent them from taking that breath, they would drown. Also, from our point of view, it was just as well they weren't too close. Sometimes we just watched with our heads out while the dolphins leapt high. One did several in a row, each leap getting higher and higher. We cheered and cheered. Some were tail-slapping. Some rose out of the water, back to back. One pair did a crossover leap in midair. The calm water was boiling with the dolphins' incredible energy, and we could hardly get our breaths, the excitement and emotion were so great.

'I noticed that about three times a dolphin let out huge bubbles like a scuba-diver's, at different intervals 4 metres down. Also some released tiny streams of bubbles from their mouths. Little eddies and whirlpools were created with the fast turning of the dolphins. These creatures were huge, but at no time did we feel concerned. They were so gentle. I never once felt any disturbance when they swam by closely.

'Most of the dolphins had very battered dorsal fins with nicks and notches in the trailing edge. One had a very notched tail fluke also. I remember one had a split in the very top of its dorsal with lots of nicks.

'We were getting a little distant from the boat, and I thought we should return. As I approached, there were several dolphins lined up just below the surface looking at the catamaran with its hydrophone and speaker dangling beneath. They appeared to be listening to the sounds. They looked quite comical from behind.

'After a while I noticed that I was shivering and thought I'd have to get out. Just then the dolphins started to leave. Raphi said he looked up, saw me getting out, and suddenly realised that he was in the water by himself. I was amazed to find that we had been in the water for 38 minutes.

'The dolphins were getting further away, so we motored up, and they came back to be with us again. Wade got in wearing his big fibreglass dolphin tail.'

Wade's Account

'Wearing my summer wetsuit, I fitted my giant monofin and slipped over the stern, followed by a red-hot eager Raphi, still shivering from his previous interlock. A group of about ten bottlenose surrounded us. I dolphined just beneath the surface at full speed. There were no juveniles present now—the rest of the tribe were up ahead. In a weaving confusion, several dolphins caromed in front of me, laying thick trails of faeces—more profusely than I had ever seen before.

'Five metres below me I saw two dolphins approach each other vertically and begin to open-jaw, alternating at each other's heads. This was not biting—the jaws never moved and the movements were gentle and reciprocal, with the occasional pass at the underside of each other's bodies. This was some sort of ritual, possibly courtship.

'Raphi and I swam side by side, arms across each other's backs. Since I could only do the dolphin-kick, Raphi was obliged to copy me, which didn't come too easy at first. Just then I saw two dolphins below us in the courtship position, one beneath the other.

'"Hey, I only wanted to show my friendship for this person, all the way from Canada." I hoped it didn't look ambiguous: perhaps a rescue attempt—so I put out thoughts of warmth towards Raphi and expected this to be conveyed by my body language.

'All this time I was putting out maximum energy, trying out the big monofin with dolphins for the first time. It provided a high speed capability, but I kept thinking of Raphi and didn't like to leave him way behind. We were some distance from the catamaran, which was still wafting towards the coast on a whisper of wind. There came a time when my body protested against the willpower driving me on. At that point the dolphins vanished into the deep blue of the late-afternoon ocean, leaving Raphi and me to plod back to the cat, dodging the strange new jellyfish that have recently appeared in the plankton, with tiny dead fish in their clutches as a warning of their power to sting quite painfully.'

Adjacent to the Poor Knights are the Pinnacles. In February 1987 Adrienne Morgan had just made a dive in the fabulous Tie Dye Arch from Steve Currie's charter boat *Masada*.

'Ten minutes after boarding the boat, Steve saw a school of 20 bottlenose dolphins a couple of hundred metres from us. I was only wearing my togs at this stage, which were a brilliant electric green. My girlfriend Carolynne was wearing bright pink. We put on mask, snorkel and fins only, quietly entered the water with about seven others, and swam towards the dolphins. The water around us echoed with their whistling, and as we swam closer, we sang and called to them. On approaching, the dolphins surrounded us, and while we duck-dived to 8 metres, spinning and twirling and whistling, they joined in. My friend Simon dived down 7 metres, spinning as he went. Dolphins followed him and played.

'Carolynne and I were lucky to be wearing bright colours; every time I duck-dived I was surrounded by whistling, frolicking dolphins, sometimes with one on each side of me. Two fizz boats nearby had divers in scuba gear who entered the water. There must have been at least 16 people in the water by now—and all our colours and noises kept the dolphins with us for an hour. I have never experienced anything as beautiful as this in my whole life. We all agreed afterwards that we felt utterly protected and secure, diving with the dolphins. If a diver was on the surface, dolphins would come and leap out of the water beside him.

'They showed immense curiosity and playfulness towards us, and it would have to be the biggest "high" I have ever had.

'After an hour, as suddenly as they had arrived, the dolphins started to leave, whistling as they went. It was all just so incredible that for as long as I live I won't forget it!'

Parallel Account by Andy Belcher

'The dolphins went berserk, not to mention the divers! While we squeaked and yahooed and dolphin-kicked, the dolphins were leaping out of the water, whizzing in and out and around us in all directions. Their favourite game appeared to be to circle around us in ever-diminishing circles, squeaking madly and nodding their heads from side to side. They seemed to single out certain divers: the more the diver tried to turn and follow the dolphin, the tighter the circle would become. We would end up dizzy, and the dolphins would move off.

'After about half an hour, as we were tiring, the dolphins began to lazily move on. But when Steve started *Masada*'s engines, and circled us, the fun began all over again. At this stage, when it looked as though the dolphins were going to stay around, we returned to the boat and loaded film into spare cameras.

'We had a total time of one hour in the water, throughout which time the dolphins were continually present and most definitely as excited as we were. They were extremely large dolphins (up to 4 metres) and although we did not notice any individual distinguishing features, some of them had a series of scratches on their backs and sides, as if someone had run an "afro" comb along them for about 10–12 centimetres. (These are teeth marks made in play by other dolphins—Wade.)

'This was all a wonderful experience, and I only hope that I don't have to wait ten years for it to happen again.'

Near the Sand Garden area at the Poor Knights in September 1987 Jeroen Jongejans was one of a party aboard *Pacific Flyer* doing scuba sea tests when bottlenose approached.

'Leaping in, we saw them very clearly, and even those aboard could hear their loud clicking sounds. The dolphins came very close around us, seven snorkellers, male and female. After ten minutes, the dolphins had moved a little further off, so *Pacific Flyer* picked us up and took us over. We were in the area east of where the two main islands meet. Prior to playing with us, the dolphins had entertained divers on board *Pacific Hideaway* for a long while.

'The second time, I noticed lots of little fish around. (I think these dolphins feed on koheru when at the Knights—Wade.) Dolphins were defecating around us frequently, in such circumstances a signal, perhaps an olfactory greeting, and coming straight for me, five at a time. Some accelerated from beneath me and leapt clear of the water. I saw several pairs mating in the vicinity. Twice, my attention was drawn to an individual.* We would play little circling games, remaining in contact for a few minutes. At one stage an older, larger dolphin came along and led my playmate away, but it returned shortly after.

'At times when the dolphins were a little further away, I found the noise of my overarm swimming brought them straight back. I used the dolphin-kick all the time, until it was just automatic, and when not too tired I would dive down. This created greater interest. After half an hour with them we were picked up by *Flyer*, quite exhausted.

'So this interlock was terminated by us motoring away with some of the dolphins accompanying us for five minutes, leaping and cavorting. Later on, divers on *Masada* and *Norseman* spent time with them, so in all I estimate those dolphins interlocked with four boatloads of people for about four hours that day—an utterly exhilarating experience.'

---

* If the diver can pick out one particular dolphin by some distinctive scar or marking and focus on this individual, he or she may find much more complex interplay develops—provided any touching is left to the dolphin. It helps if you are at full strength and feeling fit and playful.

11: Dolphin Swimming in the Hauraki Gulf

The region of the Hauraki Gulf north to the Poor Knights Islands and occasionally beyond is the home range of a tribe of very friendly, human-habituated bottlenose dolphins, at least 100 strong. There is no single location where you can be certain of meeting them, but encounters are most common around Great Barrier Island, the Mokohinau Islands, and adjacent offshore islands.

At any time, but more often in winter and early spring, divers at the Poor Knights may be lucky enough to encounter this same tribe.

Early Interlocks

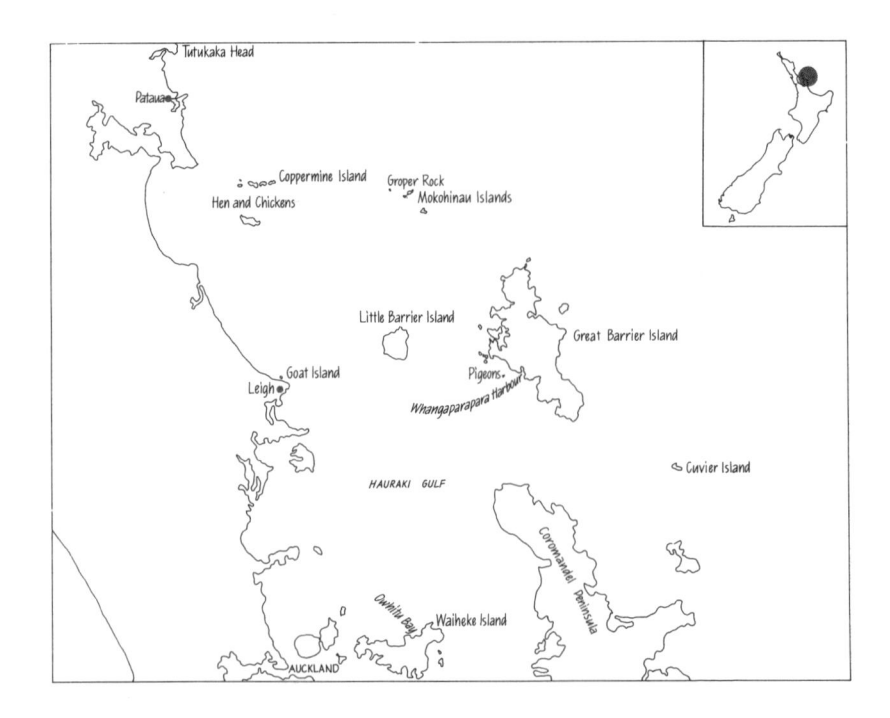

As our Project Interlock was preparing to extend itself through space with a New Zealand-wide survey of dolphin/diver encounters, I decided to go back through time and see what was going on between divers and dolphins in this country prior to the establishment of our project. From 1959 to 1975 I had published 76 editions of a magazine called *Dive*. The early diving fraternity was close-knit, and news travelled fast—especially anything exceptional, at a time when divers were constantly meeting new frontiers. But, in all that time, I found only two significant reports. As for myself and my diving friends, for the most part dolphins did not figure in our diving world other than as brief, hello-goodbye encounters.

Oddly enough, the earliest on record was from the Dolphin Underwater Club of Auckland. In Basil Cuthbert's account it seems significant that one of the divers behaved in a *communicative manner* at the outset. Note the edge of fear . . .

'On 3 January 1964, ten members of the Dolphin Underwater Club had a launch trip to the Hen and Chicken Islands. The anchor was dropped in a pleasant bay on the southern shore of the middle Chicken Island, and in no time all the divers were in the water. The day's diving was excellent, with just on 20 metres visibility, and a catch of approximately 500 kilograms of fish.

'At about five the anchor was pulled up and we headed towards the eastern Chicken Island. As we did, we noticed some dolphins playing in the strait between the Hen and Chicken Islands. We dropped anchor at the entrance to Coppermine Bay, just below the lighthouse, and three divers jumped into the water and headed ashore to dive.

'Just then it was noticed that the school had moved inshore and were heading our way. We turned on the echo sounder, hoping the high frequency sound waves would be picked up by their ultra-sensitive "ears". It seemed to work, and they started to swim our way. They came towards the boat, rolling their backs out of the water and exhaling small clouds of moist air from their blowholes. About 15 metres from the boat they dived, and looking over the side we saw them swim past in the clear water underneath the boat.

'Reg Lawson, assured by Dave Quinlan (the President) that the dolphins were harmless, jumped overboard and headed towards a large group, but he was unable to get close enough to see them underwater. Another group swam towards him, and then passed within a metre of him. He saw this lot, but their first sudden appearance so close gave him a terrific start.

'The other members, seeing Reg was not harmed, made a mad scramble for their gear, and soon there were bodies hitting the water all around the boat. The divers were Brian Currey, Gary Mcguire, Dave Quinlan, Basil Cuthbert and William McNeil.

'The splashing of the divers caused the dolphins to turn and swim back towards us. We could hear a high-pitched squeaking all around us. We were surrounded by dolphins. All of a sudden they came rushing towards us, 7 metres under the surface, travelling at a speed a shark cannot equal. The dolphins came within 2 metres of us, then peeled off in different directions and flashed away and out of sight. They were followed by more and more, coming past zooming and twisting like fighter planes in formation.

'The sight of these marine mammals—several hundred kilograms of muscle, flashing effortlessly with casual waving of their wide tails—made a diver feel like a helpless intruder, with his clumsy flippers and lack of grace. But this feeling was soon dispelled by the way these beautiful blue-and-white animals, with their ever-grinning mouths, so readily accepted us as friends and showed no fear whatsoever as they swam around us.

'We were reluctant to leave the water, and the school of 100 or more dolphins frolicked and played around us, giving a show of aquatic and aerial acrobatics, at times leaping up to 7 metres out of the water and coming down to cleave the surface with hardly a ripple.

'Several times we swam back to the boat, but each time they followed us as if they were trying to keep us with them, and so each time we turned back and carried on for a while. At last we could stay no longer, so at 6 p.m., after an hour of dolphin meeting man underwater, we climbed aboard the boat and headed back to Pataua.

'The dolphins escorted the boat, running ahead of us, leaping and playing in the bow wash, and cutting within centimetres of the bow. Suddenly our namesakes disappeared, leaving us speechless as we thought of the wonderful skin-diving experience we had undergone. But we will relive it again and again in the coloured slides and photos and in the action of hundreds of metres of movie film taken.'

The next account, also from the Hen and Chicken Islands, supports a recurrent theme in diver/dolphin stories: it seems as if one diver, searching for his partner, was guided to him by dolphins. We have parallel stories on Project Interlock files.

In December 1981 Terry Harris and Jason Lowe were seeking crays around the westernmost of the Chickens group and had become separated.

'Having caught three crayfish and being about 80 metres offshore and 18 metres deep, I turned left: bottlenose dolphins, one above the other, greeted me. After my initial start, I got the distinct impression, from their lack of activity, that they had been watching me. When spotted, they separated and were joined by about seven or eight more dolphins. One in particular swam at speed towards me on three occasions before changing direction within one and a half metres. Other dolphins were swimming around quickly in all directions, but four or five were alternately heading in a beeline for the shore, then straight back to me. I got the distinct impression they were advising me to go in that direction.

'After about three or four minutes, I "stood" on the bottom, waving my arms and squeaking. This appeared to have the desired interrogative effect, because they left . . .

'Upon the departure of the dolphins, feeling very elated, I decided to swim in the direction which the dolphins had been "showing me" and after about 40 metres came upon my partner, whom, it transpired, had not seen the dolphins, but had been looking for me.

'Upon surfacing, cries from the anchored boat informed me that I had missed a great sight of dolphins playing! They had been leaping above where I was diving.'

Cuvier Island, with its lighthouse, guards the shipping lane to Auckland Harbour.

In March 1982 police divers Mark Carrel and Peter Hawkes had just surfaced from a superb scuba-dive in clear water, enjoying the friendly fish life.

'No sooner had we taken off all our scuba gear, when a dolphin fin surfaced beside the inflatable. We looked around and could see numerous others in a large group. They would have numbered about 50. It was a mad scramble to don masks, snorkel and fins and get back into the water with these creatures.

'The tender had to pick up other divers so left us to it. We would have swum around, dolphin-dived, and generally played with them for about three-quarters of an hour. The peculiar things that we noticed about our dolphins were that they defecated close to us in a gesture that we had read from your books as being a friendly greeting sign. What was unusual and highly surprised us was that school snapper then showed no fear of us and attacked the faeces with relish. It seemed that wherever we turned there were dolphins—some large, some small, and a lot of calves hanging closely on to their mothers—moving in perfect synchronisation. The noise from these creatures was magnificent. They were calling among themselves as they came up and greeted us; however, not coming within touching distance. The only disappointing aspect of the dive was that I ran out of movie film. Despite our swimming back to the boat, the dolphins stayed with us until we got on board.

'The inflatable came around the corner soon after we got on board, trailing another large school. It appeared that the other divers on the opposite side of the island had been having similar experiences. The two schools joined together, and the combined group would have comprised about 200 dolphins. They came right back to the boat, and when the divers were on board, went out again. I grabbed spare film, jumped in the inflatable, and went back out in the hope of finding the school again.

'No sooner were we 15 metres from the boat when we seemed to be surrounded by dolphins again. I was able to film them riding the bow wave by holding the camera underwater while we were motoring along. I then jumped in and filmed some of their actions, again running out of film—my biggest curse!

'Numerous sorties were made by other divers in the inflatable, and they always managed to find the school or vice versa when they went out.

'Back on board, I loaded up my Nikonos, deciding to get some still shots. We went out, and I was to be dropped in the water. The inflatable would come back after finding the dolphins and bring them past me so I could take shots—that was the theory, anyway! I rolled over the side, and the inflatable carried on. I was setting the camera and waiting for the boat to come back, when I heard a squeal behind me and turned around to come face to face with a large dolphin hovering in the water behind me just over a metre away, as if he was playing "tag" with me. For the next 10–15 minutes I was exhilarated beyond compare by being able to dive and dolphin-kick through this large school with never-ending contact. They came closer when I was doing the dolphin-kick and actually seemed to be swimming beside me trying to teach me how to do it properly. On occasions I even saw two adult dolphins rubbing their undersides together while going through the water. Once again, numerous calves were riding shotgun with their mothers.

'It was with some reluctance that I finished my film and had to go back. I was totally rapt with the whole encounter, and if I can get the opportunity to do it again, I will. I have encountered dolphins before at the Sisters on Great Barrier, but that encounter had nothing on this one.'

Project Interlock Reply

'You are absolutely right—that interlock at Cuvier was a very high-quality one, and so much of what you describe has parallels with things that have happened to us. I have a hunch you may have met the same tribe of bottlenose dolphins that we have been meeting. I would love to see your pictures—it may be that the dolphin that hovered just behind you was Simo, who specialises in such behaviour. If any of your shots or movies show dorsal fins clearly, they would be of great value to our files.

'Some of the points you mention strike parallels:

- the snapper eating the faeces: we think snapper follow dolphins for this spin-off—your account helps to confirm our observation and is much valued.

- the approach from behind: this is a frequent manoeuvre—why do they like getting close to us when we are not expecting them? A playful ploy?
- the squeal to attract your attention is an interesting new ingredient.
- their response to your dolphin-kicking, coming closer and seeming to want to teach you, is something we have experienced, as have others who have sent in reports.

'All these parallels make your report extremely valuable, because they show this is not random behaviour and there is a pattern in their responses to various groups of divers that holds good through time and space.'

Footnote: Mark's photos confirmed he had met Simo and the dolphins we had met near the Poor Knights.

Despite their remoteness, the Mokohinaus have been a very important meeting place for humans and dolphins over the years since we first contacted Val Walters, lighthouse keeper, and learnt of her friendship with Simo, the same bottlenose dolphin we had been meeting at the Poor Knights.

In early January 1986 Roger Grace was out there on a charter yacht.

'It was late afternoon, and we were drifting in the *Taranui* about a kilometre west of Groper Rock, all lazing around in the sun and trying to hook up a shark using a deepish drifting kahawai for bait. I was hoping I might be able to get some pictures of a shark—always useful for my calendars. We had been drifting around for about an hour, when we saw a group of dolphins approaching us from the west. We rapidly threw on our snorkelling gear, and almost everyone on board went in, including John Young, the skipper. It was so calm, the boat wasn't going anywhere.

'There were about 20 bottlenose in the group, clearly visible in the 26-metres-plus visibility. Everyone had a great time playing with the dolphins, and I'm sure the dolphins enjoyed it too. There were faeces trails being released frequently: three dolphins passed in front of the camera amid a train of faeces, looking like smoke trails left by stunt aircraft. The dolphins came in to within about an arm's length of Linda, who didn't have her camera. When she dived, dolphins came zooming over to her, and on the surface they buzzed around her several times, very close.

'Slightly separated from the rest of the group, John Young saw two dolphins apparently fighting. He summoned me over, and there in the clear water about 13 metres below the surface were two dolphins standing partly up on their tails and snapping at each other, sometimes actually locking jaws and making clear "barking" noises. John and I just lay on the surface watching. It went on for at least three minutes.

'There would have been about nine people in the water and the interlock lasted about half an hour or so, after which the divers got out.

'The next day in the same area, perhaps a bit closer to Groper Rock, again late in the afternoon, we were drifting, shark fishing, when the dolphins turned up. Again several of us jumped in. I ran out of film quickly, while Linda stayed in taking some photos. I speedily changed film and jumped in again, but just then others on board saw a hammerhead about 50 metres from the boat. I had to decide whether to follow the dolphins or try for a shark shot. I chose the later, since it was harder to get the opportunity, and swam off after the shark, which was in the opposite direction from the dolphins. I swam crazily about, following orders from the boat, but of course never saw the shark. When I returned to the boat, the dolphins had gone.'

Great Barrier Island is another important area for dolphin encounters. Just five days after Roger Grace's experience, Lyn Baynham met some bottlenose there.

'My husband, Ted, and I had just surfaced from a dive at the Pigeons, and were pulling our anchor, when we noticed a large school of dolphins about a kilometre further out to sea and several kilometres towards Whangapara.

'We headed their way immediately, and they came up to us very readily, rolling over and looking up at us hanging over the side of the boat. One performed several leaps right out of the water up to the level of our flying bridge, on occasions having us believe he was trying to hitch a ride. Four others formed a line across our bow and swam in the same formation with us, regardless of our speed or direction. Their sounds were very audible, and every few minutes one would "blow", showering us thoroughly, break away, then regroup with the other three. We counted up to 30 dolphins around the boat; there were far more, but they did not approach.

'We stopped the boat so two of us aboard could enter the water. The dolphins stayed very close by and were curious enough to make several passes beneath and beside us, singly and in pairs. They were all large adult dolphins, no babies being evident. Two of them made several passes close by and seemed to be supporting a third, who defecated within 2 metres of me as they passed. My husband, who was watching from the boat, called out that to him it seemed they were supporting one that was wounded, but they went by me in the water several times in this manner and I could see no injuries. The dolphin that appeared to be supported by the others then left of its own accord. The other two stayed, and up to five others were passing beneath me constantly, sometimes rolling over to look at me. Two snorkellers were in the water with me experiencing many similar close encounters. The dolphins made no move to leave us and stayed with the boat for half an hour after we left the water.

'They then followed the boat almost to the Pigeons, riding our bow wave and squeaking loudly.

'We had made no attempts to touch them and noticed that they approached us quite readily, regardless of what kick we were using, or whether we were moving or stationary.

'We were totally exhilarated after this encounter, and had a feeling that we had been thoroughly checked out by these dolphins, who seemed to be quite happy to let us decide when to break off.'

Goat Island Encounters

Goat Island at Leigh is an immensely popular Marine Reserve where many people explore unexploited reef life, others receive scuba-diving lessons, and young marine scientists pursue their studies.

For bottlenose dolphins it is a popular calling place during their travels around the Hauraki Gulf. For these reasons, encounters are quite frequent.

In March 1980 Owen Carter and his companion Rob Orms had an encounter that impressed them deeply.

'We were on scuba going north around the easternmost point. Rob had surfaced to choose a course and indicated for me to surface as well. He pointed out the approaching dolphins heading straight for us. I immediately dived to around 9 metres and met five or six, who split at the last moment and passed either side of me. They then turned and swam back under me until they had just gone out of sight. Visibility was approximately 12 metres. Unreal! They came straight back, split either side of me, and swam back under me to about the limit of visibility. This was repeated about four times. I was ecstatic to be able to swim with them and have them come back. Other dolphin encounters have always been short-lived, at a greater distance, with just glimpses of shadowy forms speeding through the dull curtain underwater. Because of this and to some extent because of reading your Interlock reports, I made no effort to touch them, but devoted my energy to swimming with a dolphin-kick, doing barrel rolls and loops, and also vocalising squeaks and whistles. In other words, I tried to hold their interest and establish some sort of rapport. Rob later revealed that he thought I had gone mad and could not understand why I was behaving like that at all. On reflection, I wonder if the dolphins think something similar: "It looks human but does not act like it."

'When they left me after the fourth or fifth approach, I started to surface towards Rob, feeling tired, but before reaching him he signalled their return. The pattern of the previous meeting was repeated—passing me closely one way, a quick turn and passing back out underneath me, then another turn about 12 metres away for the repeat run; four or five runs and then away out of sight for a while. The total encounter comprised perhaps five such meetings, each involving four or five runs. It seemed to last forever, but it can not have been all that long.

'In discussing the encounter with non-diving friends, it was suggested that the pattern seemed to indicate that the dolphins wanted me to go with them out to sea. The long leg of the passes was out to the sea—eastward. This interpretation of their behaviour, as "attempted" communication by them has left me wondering. It never crossed my mind that they were trying to do or say anything at the time. How's that for not thinking about the situation? If possible, I would be interested to hear your views on this encounter and how it fits in with other encounters.'

Wade's Reply

'As to the significance of what the dolphins did, I feel you are on the right track in just enjoying the experience. I think they know we are incapable of keeping up with them. The experience may have a significance in time: you and Rob will never be quite the same again and will perhaps develop a greater rapport with cetaceans from that day. Thus, their manoeuvres were a significant form of body language that clearly told you those dolphins were interested in you, trusted you, and that it was not the sort of meeting you could expect to have with a fish. So it did have a degree of communication. I hope you may enjoy more.'

At Goat Island in August 1985 Michaela Webb was doing her sea test and had just removed her mask as instructed, when dolphins appeared.

'After clearing my mask, I opened my eyes to a grey mass flashing past my face. Immediately I thought 'Shark!' but on calming myself found a group of three or four dolphins circling us. We circled with them, keeping the dolphins in view. They disappeared for brief moments and returned with a couple more dolphins each time. Eventually we had a school of about six to eight adult dolphins circling us. They were all longer than us, at least 3 metres in length, and swam within touching distance. At one stage I reached out to touch one of these sleek, graceful animals, but changed my mind in case I frightened them away. My buddy was dolphin-kicking and moving up to the dolphins. They disappeared after about three to four minutes but returned for a brief visit and were gone again.

'The three of us surfaced and called to the other instructor and students. Unfortunately they were too far away to hear us properly. For me it was a big buzz, specially since it was my first sea dive.'

One Saturday morning in August 1993 Leigh Marine Laboratory technician Brady Doak got a call to say there was a group of bottlenose dolphins heading along the coast towards Goat Island.

'I arrived at the laboratory to find three students, Joe, Brent and Jasmine, waiting in their wetsuits. I told them to take their snorkel gear and climb down the ladder to the reef. The dolphins were now within easy swimming range in the entrance to the channel.

'Meanwhile I assembled camera gear, four scuba sets, outboard, etc. and met them in the channel with the boat.

'I slipped into the water, with camera and scuba, and was instantly surrounded by an excited group of dolphins whistling and zooming close, wriggling with excitement. They appeared to have been reacting to the snorkellers and were in a playful, exuberant mood. The divers swam to the boat to grab their scuba equipment. We all spent the next hour with the dolphins. I was trying to film them, so my attention was divided. I was, however, aware of two or three dolphins with distinctive marks or dorsal nicks who repeatedly swam close, within a metre. Numbers of the group were difficult to estimate, but there would probably have been 10 to 15 directly involved in the immediate area. Snapper were evident in the water column throughout the encounter.

'We eventually got out when the groups moved on down the coast towards Cape Rodney. We followed them in the boat. Jasmine and Brent entered the water again. However, it was evident that the dolphins had played enough, as they took no further interest in the divers.'

Jasmine Hansen's Account

'In between the gentle hush of leaves rustling on branches, you could hear the rhythmic jingle of the sea rippling onto the shore.

'The sun glittered across the water, mirroring the distinct silhouette of Goat Island at Leigh Marine Reserve. Birds all around were rising and singing to this glorious day.

'As I sat absorbing the morning warmth, something caught my eye. From the balcony of Leigh Laboratory I had a brilliant bird's-eye view of the channel below. There—I saw it again! Yes! There are more. "Dolphins! There are dolphins in the channel!" And with that everything slid into hysteria. My body was gushing with adrenalin as I ran to the gear shed. Struggling with wetsuits, booties and hoods, Brent and Jo joined me, both as exhilarated as I.

'"Just go down with snorkel gear and keep them entertained, and I'll bring the rest of the gear," called Brady. He opened the hatch to a very long ladder descending the cliff onto the rocks below.

'Calm now, step by step—that ladder seemed to go on forever. My footing wasn't fast enough for the eagerness of wanting to get down: on landing I slipped on the rocks—ouch!

'Fins on and we leapt in. It was a fairly decent swim out to where they were leaping and playing, but I seemed to walk on water and was there in a second.

'The dolphins shone like royal silver in the sunlight as they came up for air. The water was slightly murky from the previous night's storm, so you could hear them before you could see them. A series of high-pitched beeps as they talked among themselves—it sounded almost like a playground full of kids squealing with excitement. Huge grey torpedoes zoomed towards me, merging into fins and the distinct shape of dolphins. They were very curious. Their elegance underwater amazed me—so gentle and smooth—it's no wonder dive gear is becoming more and more similar to the streamlined shape of the dolphin. We were clearly inferior with our clunky gear and slow manoeuvrability. Still, the dolphins seemed to like us all the same.

'We were circled by at least 30 big bottlenose dolphins. A few were noticeably cheeky, heading straight for my face and veering at the last minute. It was a game to see which one could get the closest. I felt like I was in the middle of a game of "chicken". I imitated their rolls and flips, which seemed to excite them even more; I felt they knew we were trying to communicate. Our gymnastic stunts got faster and more complex as the dolphins played along.

'One particular dolphin stood out remarkably: he had a series of big scratches down his back and was always there—everywhere I turned he was showing off.

'The circle game was definitely the favourite: stomach to belly we swam round and round in circles, getting faster and faster.

'At the surface I spotted Jo and Brent, who were screaming at the top of their voices "Yahoo!" as some leapt out of the water performing acrobatic flips. Everywhere I looked were these amazing living torpedoes. The permanent smiles of the beautiful wise dolphins surrounded me again, and with them, the orchestral language. Scratchy was definitely the cheekiest one, as he bunted a floating piece of seaweed towards me. Grabbing it, I threw it back. Again it would get nudged towards me. This was incredible; it was obvious that this was a game he was playing. The seaweed got pushed around a few more times before Scratchy shot off for a game of hide and seek, with me in fast pursuit. They were definitely the most beautiful and intelligent creatures in the water!

'There was a mother and her newborn calf who kept their distance, and what appeared to be a couple, who remained side by side the whole time, swimming slowly and peacefully—as if in love. Their gracefulness overwhelmed me. I did not feel threatened in the slightest, nor they by me. I think it was an unspoken understanding that we were just there to play, like them.

'As the grey torpedoes flashed past and circled, it struck me that these are animals that are slaughtered by the hundreds and caught in nets all around the world every year. I found it hard to come to terms with the fact that we think we are the superior species and have the right to kill these exquisite animals. Under the water we are clumsy, slow, unaware and weak; the dolphin is by far the superior.

'My air supply was pretty low so I headed back to the boat. Without scuba gear, we had a lot more flexibility and flips were so much easier. Brent had it down to a fine art as I watched him corkscrew down to the bottom like a ballerina in a dance. We imitated everything the dolphins did—"Simon says" was now "Scratchy says".

'We had been in the water now for about two and a half hours, and I had swum kilometres without feeling a muscle in my body working. The total thrill of such an experience overrode everything else. The dolphins seemed to have settled right down, and the novelty of the games had worn off. Wearily we climbed back on the boat—exhausted, both mentally and physically.

'As we motored back to shore, I still couldn't believe what had just happened—I had swum, played, even communicated with dolphins, a long-lived childhood dream that I share with many other people.

'For the rest of the day I kept my eyes peeled on the channel, on the edge of my seat. Every ripple and shadow made my heart leap out my throat. But the dolphins had left for the day.'

Four days later Jasmine and Brady sighted the same bottlenose dolphins close in against the rocks near the eastern point of Goat Island. This time there was no play—the dolphins were very busy feeding. Brady wrote:

'As we moved around the seaward coast heading north, we came upon a small inlet in the back of which stood a sea cave. The dolphins were herding kahawai into the bay and forcing them into the cave, which was so full of fish that they were being forced up out of the water in a boiling mass. The dolphins were feeding on them. By the time we had anchored in the inlet, the dolphins had moved on, but it took some time for the fish to venture out. We were able to swim into the cave among them. I noticed a stunned kahawai on the bottom. It was still breathing but drifted upside down and appeared to be bruised and scaled. We did not see the dolphins again and went on with our dive.

'Jasmine told me she had seen a dolphin with the same body markings as on the first encounter.'

Waiheke Dolphin: Fish Giver

Late one day in January 1989 a fleet of five small yachts, travelling in convoy, anchored at Owhiti Bay, Waiheke Island. Four launches already shared the bay. Rachael Caplan leads off with an account of a bottlenose dolphin that behaved in an extraordinary way, running through so many play patterns that solitary dolphins manifest—but never quite like this!

'We had been anchored for about an hour when a dolphin swam into the bay. Noticing the very pockmarked fin, we watched her swim very close to *Taitua*, where she dropped a trevally from her mouth as if presenting it. The head had been in the dolphin's mouth and was squashed, but the rest of the fish was unmarked. It was later smoked on the beach. All the launch crews were ashore having a barbecue, but when the dolphin was sighted most of the young ones took to the water, along with most of our yacht crews, to swim with her. She would swim very close but did not like to be touched, and would visit each boat in turn, looking at us, then diving under and around each boat.

'We lost sight of her as darkness came. She may have been in the bay all night, but we could not see.

'At about 7.30 next morning we watched the dolphin swim into the bay, *once again with a fish!* This time she was bobbing it along with her nose, and it looked fairly stunned. She reached the bow of *Quid Non*, let it go, and swam under the boat. The fish lay on top of the water for a few seconds, then must have "come to", as it took off, obviously thankful for its reprieve.

'For the rest of the morning, until ten, when we set out for home, the dolphin stayed with us in the bay, occasionally going over to visit another boat anchored at the end of the bay. Jane Leyland got in their dinghy and rowed all over the bay, and wherever she went the dolphin followed—so if we wanted a closer look all we had to do was call Jane over and sure enough the dolphin came too. About mid-morning the dolphin went to each boat in turn and rubbed her nose up and down the anchor warp. Whether this meant anything more than an itchy nose I don't know, but it seemed like a friendly gesture.'

Geoff Leyland's Account: Day Two

'At about seven I woke up with Dad telling me there was a dolphin in the bay. I think then that if my bunk had been slightly larger and easier to get in and out of I would have flown out of bed. I got into my togs and wetsuit in record time. Then I paused, "looking for the dolphin", but was really trying to get over my nervousness as no-one else was in yet.

'For about the first five or ten minutes in the water I was alone with the dolphin and followed it shyly around the bay. Then Dad joined me, but I was surprised at the reluctance of people to get in the water. Dad and I swam around after the dolphin for some time. The dolphin was obviously interested in us—it wasn't jumping, it took no notice of boats, and it was alone. At first we just followed the dolphin around, mostly in shallow water—and every time we couldn't keep up, the dolphin would come back and get us. If we just lay on the surface, the dolphin would swim in circles under us on its side, watching us. It didn't seem to be part of the game to follow it under the water or get too close to it, and when I did touch it, lightly, the dolphin took off, and I felt guilty about that.

'Mum was the next person to get in and she swam around with us for a while. The dolphin was obviously wanting us to play a following game, because when we couldn't keep up it would come back and get us. I'm afraid that none of us could swim fast enough to be exciting. Mum and Dad eventually got out, and Conrad, Barclay and Giles came in.

'At this time we noticed that the dolphin was carrying seaweed, so we started to look for things for it to play with. We tried life rings at first, but this provoked no reaction, and then Frisbees with the same result, although we did have some fun with the Frisbees. We tried offering seaweed to the dolphin but didn't think of carrying it ourselves.

'After about two hours I got out and had breakfast. To our amazement the dolphin seemed to wait for us. It was swimming around and around very slowly in a small circle, breathing once every round. At some time during the day, Rachael Cameron on *Quid Non* saw the dolphin playing with a fish. It had apparently caught quite a large kahawai by stunning it and was letting it go and catching it again.

'As soon as I had finished breakfast, I got into the dinghy and started to row around. The dolphin really enjoyed this, because I could row fast enough to be some fun, and we played a chasing game all around the corner of the bay we were in. I would row as fast as I could, with the dolphin following, then I'd suddenly turn and go in another direction, keeping this up until I got too tired. During the game, the dolphin came quite close into the beach, and several times I tried jumping out of the dinghy to see if it would come right up to someone in shallow water—but it didn't want to. The dolphin seemed quite intrigued with dinghies and enjoyed following them around, and once it scratched on my oar.

'When a boat came into the bay, the dolphin raced out to meet it, faster than I could row after it, and really gave the people on board a surprise. They motored over to me to "give me a thrill" but didn't seem to understand when I told them that we had been swimming with it for *two hours* and that they should jump in straight away. At first the dolphin went to see this new boat in the bay, but no-one would swim with it, or even row after it, so it quickly came back. After another boat came in and failed to do anything interesting, Mum decided that she had to do something and rowed over to get it back. In fact Mum had quite a lot of fun "taking" the dolphin from boat to boat. When she "took" the dolphin to snorkellers, it tended to swim around them and meet the dinghy on the other side. My windsurfing board created even more interest . . .'

12: Swimming with Bay of Plenty Dolphins

From Coromandel Peninsula, south around East Cape to Mahia Peninsula, there is an enormous sweep of coastline that offers excellent diving opportunities, and for that reason, superb dolphin contacts have developed.

The earliest on file is of very high quality. For some reason David Harvey and his friend Frank Long did not react with as much fear as is evident in subsequent early reports, but there was an edge of uncertainty.

David had been scuba-diving for two years, basically a pot hunter, until that calm, perfect day at the end of October 1978, when he set out for Rabbit Island after launching the runabout at Whangamata. At the end of the day David wrote in his diary:

'Today something really strange, almost mystic, happened. The experience has given me a respect for the sea, for the life in the ocean.

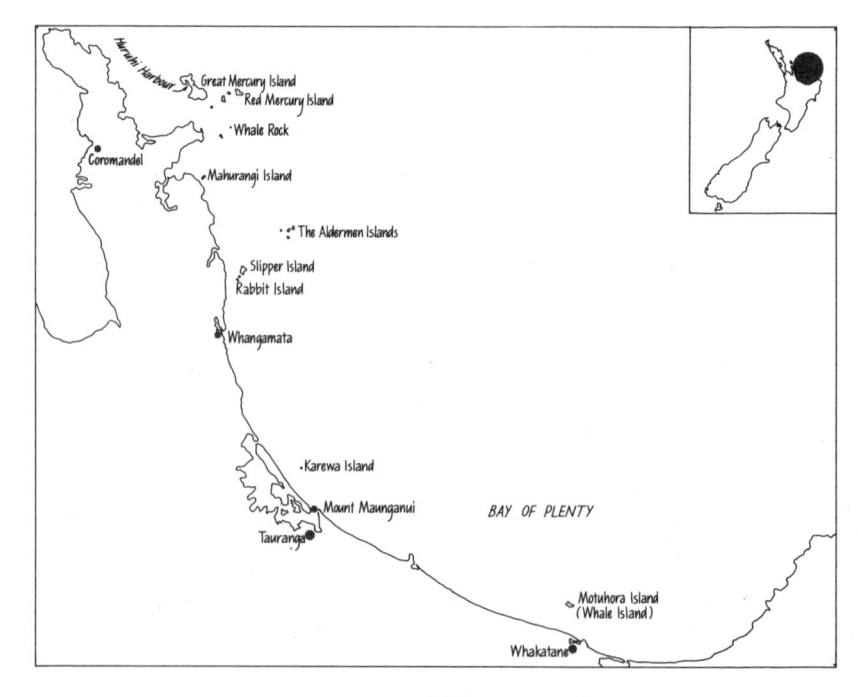

Somehow spearing fish and chasing crays seems a bit pointless now. The desire has completely gone, to be replaced with a yearning to know more about the sea and what makes it tick.

'We were about 3 kilometres out of Whangamata and a kilometre offshore when Frank Long touched my arm and pointed ahead. "Dolphins," he said. I looked ahead, and there, about 300 metres away, I could see dark fins breaking the surface of the water. "What do you reckon," said Frank. "Get a closer look?"

'"Sure," I said. We were in no particular rush. We had all day. Frank headed the boat slightly to port, because the dolphins were travelling across our path. As the motor ate up the distance, I could see the sun glinting off the backs of the animals as they arched out of the water. I was a little disappointed, because I thought that dolphins jumped right out of the water as they travelled. Perhaps these ones were a bit lazy. They weren't in any hurry. Their dorsal fins came slowly out of the water, described a casual arc in the air, and disappeared back under. Their movements were very precise and measured. A funny thing was that they didn't seem too disturbed by our approach. They must have been able to hear the sound of the motor—I think I read somewhere that they have very good hearing. We were about 50 metres away from them, when Frank suddenly gave the motor full throttle, and then cut the power completely, allowing the boat's momentum to carry us towards the herd. We could see them very clearly now, and we could hear them too. They hardly made a sound as they broke surface, save for a slight whoosh as they breathed. The boat drifted to a halt.

'"Shall we give them something to think about?" said Frank.

'"Like what?" I asked.

'"Hop in with them."

'"Do you think we should?" I ventured.

'"Why not. They're harmless. Besides, I've wanted to see what they look like underwater."

'"Do you think we have enough air?" I asked. We only had enough for two dives.

'"Use snorkels," he said. "They're on the surface."

'I felt pretty reluctant about the whole idea. I know dolphins are friendly, but one never knows. The only dolphins I'd seen had been at Marinelands, and they were trained. Wild dolphins were another matter. Anyway, I agreed to go over with him, so we put on our buoyancy compensators and weight belts and got ready to hop in. As I sat on the gunwale of the boat, I saw one of the dolphins leave the herd and head towards us. It was a fairly impressive sight, as it arched along and at a pretty good speed too, whooshing air each time as it broke the surface.

'It came straight at the bow, and about 4 metres from the boat it moved slightly to its right and swam along side. I saw it flash under me—

all 3 metres of it. That was a big dolphin. The water was so clear that I could see all its features—snout, eyes, blowhole, tail—everything. And in that mouth were a large number of very sharp teeth, and the snout was what it used for ramming sharks. Yes, I *was* afraid, but Frank called the "let's go" signal and I kept my fear down and my snorkel mouthpiece in and fell backwards over the side. Frank came up under the boat, and we looked for the herd. There they were—about 10 metres away and to the left. We let the boat drift—there was no wind or swell, and we probably wouldn't be away long.

'We finned towards the herd, and I suppose our breathing through snorkels sounded pretty much like air from a dolphin's blowhole. Something attracted me—a movement from the corner of my eye. There was this same fellow who had come alongside, swimming back to the herd. His movements were so easy and graceful, and now I could just see the curve of a smile that dolphins have on their snouts.* All of a sudden I lost my initial fear. Perhaps it was because that smile was so innocent and friendly; I felt that I had to get closer to these animals. As I swam towards them, popping my head out of the water to see if I was heading in the right direction, I could hear a curious sound, a clicking, clacking noise, with strange little chirps as well. I'd never heard the noise before, and after a while I worked it out. It was the dolphins.

'Then it happened. We saw them. Talk about "now you see them, now you don't". It was amazing! Fantastic! Earlier we had seen their fins and backs from the surface. Now we could see what happened as they went under. In almost military formation those dolphins that had surfaced arched smoothly down for about 7 metres, and as they did so, other dolphins went to the surface for air. There were twice as many in the water as we thought. And they were big too. They were a sort of slate grey on top, which gradually faded to a sort of cream underneath. And they all had that crazy smile. The noise increased as we approached, and it was obvious that we were responsible.

'Suddenly, one of the dolphins broke away from its comrades, who were all diving, and did an amazing thing. He stood on his tail and hung in the water! His head came around, and he looked straight at us and slowly moved his head from side to side. Then he stopped this and looked at us again. We heard a different succession of clicks and squeaks as he did this. We looked at him, and he looked at us. A moment later he was joined by another dolphin, and another. I felt a little apprehensive.

---

* While dolphins are undoubtedly benign towards humans, the dolphin 'smile' is a recurrent theme that needs comment. The upcurved mouth of a dolphin is simply an aspect of its anatomy and is in no way an expression of emotion. This fixed 'smile' remains, even when humans are harpooning them. Is a bulldog permanently miserable?

'Perhaps they were lining up for a charge. Remembering that the best form of defence is offence, I took a large gulp of air and headed down to about 5 metres, and hung there for a moment. Then I swam towards the three dolphins. They didn't move. Frank came down alongside, and we got within 3 metres of them, when they headed for the surface, and so did we, maintaining visual contact with them. At the surface, we emptied our snorkels, then went down again. So did our three friends, squeaking and chattering madly. The sound became white noise. I'm sure the others were joining in. To me, anyway, it sounded as if the dolphins were surprised.

'We surfaced again, and as we did so a wonderful thing happened. One of the three, probably the first one who stood on his tail, swam towards us, stopped level with our face masks at a distance of a metre, squeaked once, loudly, and dived below us. I couldn't believe it. I shot up to the surface. So did Frank. It was fantastic, wonderful! We raved madly—speaking nonsense. An overwhelming sensation of friendship possessed us both—friendship for the dolphin, for each other, for everyone and everything. In that instant, for some reason, everything became beautiful, vibrant, and indescribably sacred. I felt as if I were on the verge of discovering the secret of life itself. And all because of an inquisitive dolphin. We went down again, and watched them. We swam closer to them, or tried to, but they frustrated us by maintaining a distance that was near enough for us to observe them, but far enough away to be tantalising. It was almost as if they were leading us—and they were, for we followed, up and down, up and down.

'I don't know how long we stayed with them, but we didn't get any closer. The effort of diving, surfacing, clearing the snorkel, inhaling, and going straight down again was very taxing. We began to tire, and so we decided to head for the boat. We surfaced, inflated our compensators, and looked for the boat. We had gone in a semicircle, and the boat was 300 metres away. We struck out slowly. But we had no regret.'

The next report comes from Mahia Peninsula, where in November 1979 two small boats were anchored on a flat calm sea about a kilometre offshore. Divers were resting after a deep dive, having lunch and doing some water-skiing. This account is valuable because it shows that there was a time when divers really feared dolphins. Our newsletters in diving and boating magazines would have helped to overcome this, leading to ever richer encounters.

Graeme Thomson Relates

'One of the guys was playing around down below in about 7 metres of water on scuba, feeding fish, and we were all watching him. We had seen the common dolphin herd quite a distance away, but they were on the move so we didn't go over. All of a sudden three or four broke off from the herd and shot directly towards this poor guy below. They covered the last 80 metres in a single breath at incredible speed; each one did a complete circle around him and then, just as quick, took off back to the herd. While this happened, there was an almighty cloud of bubbles, a Polaris-powered diver, a scream that had something to do with copulation, and our brave diver appeared.'

Mike Amphlett, his wife and another couple were anchored in Huruhi Harbour, Great Mercury Island, late in December 1979. When they awoke, it was raining, so the men decided to dive for scallops. Note that human fear was close at hand . . .

'My friend, an experienced scuba-diver, dived down in about 8 metres of water to check if there were any scallops on the bottom. He returned with a few, so I got a sack, put on my scuba gear, and joined him in the water. After checking the keel of our trailer yacht, we swam to the bottom and collected some scallops. We were having a general exploration, when a large grey object swam past me. It was so close that I couldn't see exactly what it was. I might add that this was only my third dive in the ocean, and that I am new at the sport. I immediately thought it was a shark, and as you can probably imagine, in my fright, I nearly filled my wetsuit!

'It was not until they circled us that we realised that it was not one but three bottlenose dolphins—two large ones and a baby. They circled us for a few minutes at a distance of about 2 metres. They seemed very inquisitive, their heads moving about, looking at us from every angle in a fashion similar to a seagull. We were a bit unsure of our feelings, having these creatures so near, but were reassured, having read various articles on the dolphin family and their friendly natures. With one final look at us, they then swam away. The visibility was about 5 metres.

'I thought the best thing to do was go back to the boat, but after looking over to my friend, I saw that he was carrying on gathering scallops, so I decided to do likewise. All of a sudden the dolphins reappeared. They circled us as before for a few seconds, being generally nosy, and then seemed to head seawards.

'We gathered up our scallops and headed back to the yacht about 18 metres away. When we surfaced, we saw the women on board having a thoroughly entertaining time watching the dolphins from the safety of the boat. I heard them laughing. It was not until I was back on board that I learnt that one of the dolphins had swum upside down between my friend's legs, brushing his chest as it passed by. The women ribbed us for not playing with the dolphins, who had shown that they wanted to.

'Soon after, a large trimaran passed close by, and the dolphins took after it. They circled it and to our amazement started a floor show by jumping vertically out of the water to a height of about 4 metres. They made four jumps, just like the ones you would see at a Marineland show. The trimaran started circling to keep the dolphins jumping, but the dolphins circled a few more times and then headed out to sea.'

Whale Island Dolphins

Commencing in August 1979, Ramari ('Dusty') Stewart and Des Crossland set up a second Project Interlock dolphin research base on Whale Island, 5 kilometres out from Whakatane in the Bay of Plenty. For a year they studied a common dolphin pod living in the vicinity, using *Interlock II*, a small sailing catamaran—a miniature replica of our own—and similar methods to those Project Interlock had developed in the Poor Knights area, 400 kilometres to the north.

To our delight, Ramari and Des identified dolphins we had seen, evidence of considerable coastal movement in summer. They found that some common dolphins were resident in the area all year around, whereas in our study area they left in winter.

'Most of the dolphins we encounter are on the seaward side of Whale Island,' wrote Ramari. 'We see scouts racing inside the island, but the main population keeps to the north. Each time we circle the island clockwise. Whenever I sight them, I use my whistle. If they are heading away, they will turn and come over. They have not yet come to us when we have simply sighted them.'

27 September 1979: 'The day we first met games initiator Paleface, three dolphins were performing complex patterns between our bows. We were stationary. One dolphin would appear close to the surface, and then, as if a bud were unfolding from below, there would be three petals—just like that drawing Maori elder Dan Tana showed us.

'We love the boat, as we are so close to the water from all points. Today I lay on deck, arm outstretched in the water. Dolphins approached and audibly "buzzed" my hand. For an hour we stayed almost stationary with a group of 15 while the main group was nearby, spread over an area of about 5 kilometres.'

7 October 1979: 'When we were passing the Boulder Bank, we were joined by four mothers and their young. Each baby was the same size, just a few months old. Whether the mother was shooting our bows or lying still on the surface, her offspring never left her side. We could not locate the main group. Then, a lone dolphin stuck its head out at the stern and raced off north. It was Paleface.'

12 October 1979: 'Five kilometres off the northwestern point of the island we met 12 adult dolphins—all with identifiable fins. Immediately they came on our bows.

'Des was at the tiller when two dolphins appeared, one positioned off each rudder. Whenever he turned the rudders, they synchronised their movements. Later, one of this pair turned upside down at the surface and gazed up through the two hulls. I was on the port bow, forward of the deck, and peeped under at him. Des and I burst out laughing when this dolphin turned right side up and somehow sculled backwards for about 6 metres, curving right around until his tail was to our stern.'

13 October 1979: 'About a kilometre off the northwestern point of the island, we spotted them. The main group was hunting, spread over an area of several kilometres. There was a big group of teenagers who cavorted with us. They were visited by one or two adults, who periodically joined in. One was Paleface. The wind was gusting. We set our course for the east end of the island, and the teenage group came home with us most of the way. Because we had our outboard going, they would sound at the stern to avoid it, and pop up under the deck. They kept racing out after the two adults, whenever they left the group, and then returned to continue the game. It was as if they were having a ball, but had to race off from time to time to make sure it was all right.'

On 15 December 1979 Ramari and Des left Whakatane River at seven in the morning. Just off the entrance they met 15 familiar common dolphins, all with newborn babies, some only hours old, just off the entrance. For two and a half hours they accompanied their catamaran, cruising slowly along the coast.

The following Sunday they met this same group of mothers and babies again. As soon as they changed from motor to sail, the babies, brimming with vitality, all came between the hulls, with their mothers on either side of the vessel, while Ramari played the flute to them.

During their study year, Ramari and Des gathered valuable recognition data for dozens of common dolphins and learnt much about this resident pod.

In February 1993 this area was to become part of a Whakatane-based dolphin-swim operation, initiated by people involved in New Zealand's first such business at Kaikoura. The work of Ramari and Des was already well known.

It was midwinter 1980 when ten divers of the Auckland University Underwater Club encountered a group of about 15 common dolphins at the Mercury Islands. They were diving from the *Whai* at Whale Rock when the dolphins came near the boat.

Writes Gary Tee:

'They were leaping playfully, some performing backwards somersaults. I leant over the bow to watch them squeaking loudly and rolling over to look up at me. When the boat stopped, they noticed eight snorkellers nearby and went across to play with them. For about half an hour the dolphins cavorted among the swimmers, squeaking excitedly and rolling on their sides to gaze up at them. Whenever the swimmers tried to stroke them, the dolphins wriggled aside to avoid contact. After 20 minutes they moved away, but as our people were returning to the boat the dolphins returned for another ten minutes' play.'

In June 1982 a pod of 20 common dolphins appeared on the seaward side of Rabbit Island off Mt Maunganui and proceeded slowly around the southern end of the island into shallow water over sand, passing along the ocean beach to the harbour entrance off North Rock, where they remained in loose assembly for over an hour.

John Crossman joined the school on snorkel by intercepting their course of travel.

'On making contact, each member of the school passed beneath or close by—rolling on its side to investigate me before passing on into the gloom. (Visibility was less than 5 metres.)

'The initial contact occurred in shallow water. A number of dolphins defecated in my field of vision, and after their passing the water in my vicinity was a mass of faeces. Compliment or insult?

'There were a number of young present—being very closely shepherded. They came by me in the presence of a parent, presumably, literally "tucked under a wing". There was plenty of noise and communication. Although I was close enough to have touched several as they passed, there was no indication on their part of any real interest in me apart from initial investigation each time I re-established contact. Visibility was so poor that it was impossible to establish their behaviour or level of interest, apart from the close passes, beyond 5 metres.

'They put on a real display of jumping, tail-standing in the harbour entrance, before continuing on towards Karewa Island to the northwest.'

On the most perfect of diving days in early February 1986 Thelma Wilson had already made two scuba-dives at Red Mercury Island.

'I had just commented to David and Andrew about what a perfect day it had been, although I would have loved to have seen some dolphins, when David spotted movement at the southeastern end of the island . . . whales, we thought. The guys had seen orca the previous day.

'On motoring over in our boat, we found a large school of bottlenose dolphins—their size really surprised me. I'm not sure how many there were—30 at least—I could not count with my head in the cabin, hurriedly grabbing mask, snorkel and fins. Andrew steered around the shore in the middle of one group, while David and I dropped over the side.

'First thought—what a noise, an incredible racket—whistling and squeaking and clicking at full volume. The office Christmas party has nothing on those guys.

'So, I was floating in the water, beside a 3-metre long mammal, trying to make intelligent-sounding squeaks and clicks through a snorkel, and feeling somewhat like the ugly duckling. They were so sleek and aerodynamic in the water that when they blasted past me only a metre away I felt very little disturbance. Their underneaths were a pale creamy colour, their backs and fins a dark grey. Some were swimming belly to belly—possibly mating. Until we hit the water, they seemed to be feeding amid tiny shrimp-like bugs, of which there were millions, but they were obviously curious about us and our behaviour. I did a couple of somersaults—my two closest dolphin companions copied. I did another one—so did they. Then one nosed right up close and chuckled at me— a chuckle is a chuckle, no matter what language it is in. I felt like smiling, and felt he was smiling back. In fact they just felt so friendly! We did barrel rolls, more somersaults and dives, my companions outmanoeuvring me each time.

'They cruised off to investigate the boat. Another group of dolphins then made us the centre of their attention. When there were none close by, slapping my fins on the surface soon brought them crowding back. Although at times out of sight, they were always audible.

'With one dolphin I was struck by the expression in its eye—first because it was an expression. I'm used to looking at fish underwater, but not a 'scientist' eyeing me up to determine age, sex, size and speed. There really was someone home in there! Seals, which I've often swum with, can put across facial expressions, but this creature was into eye contact. He probably learnt more about me than I did about him.

'After about half an hour of such cordial company and strenuous snorkelling, one dolphin started circling me and had me a little concerned. He seemed a bit larger than the others and was circling very closely and fast, and each time I left the surface he barrelled over the top of me then leapt out of the water, coming down with tremendous force—easily enough to squash me if he miscued his act. On getting back into the boat, Andrew commented he thought I was about to be raped by a dolphin—which is what had also crossed my mind.

'As they regrouped and headed on their way—northwest—we warmed up back in the boat, still buzzing with joy. An unforgettable day.'

In early October 1986 a party of divers aboard a charter launch were anchored at the Aldermen Islands, off the Coromandel coast. They were having lunch after a dive, when a large group of bottlenose dolphins swam into the bay and approached their boat.

'Despite the efforts of four divers,' wrote Fred Pavitt, who quickly donned snorkel gear, 'the dolphins continued on past. They milled about on the far side of the bay about a kilometre away, appearing to be very close inshore and playing with some craypot buoys.

'Half an hour after first sighting the dolphins, we started the launch for our next dive. This attracted the attention of a small group of dolphins who headed towards us. Eight snorkellers entered the water and managed a good contact with this small group.

'These dolphins were very vocal, and it appeared to those in the water that they may have summoned the larger group, as we were soon surrounded by dolphins—about 30 were counted from the boat—all of whom were friendly and interested in the divers. Many of the dolphins would approach a diver, seem to halt while being curious, then move slowly off, while others would flash past quickly, close enough to cause some concern initially.

'When we dived down to the dolphins, some of those on board were wondering about the sanity of their buddies, as we were imitating the dolphin squeaks to hold their attention. Dolphins would glide in front of us and defecate directly in our path. All the dolphins were covered in fresh marks, as though they had been scratching on rocks before joining us. None of the divers in the water noticed any identifying features on them, but some of the older dolphins were with their young.

'The encounters seemed to us all to be over far too quickly, but when we returned to the boat we found we had been in the water for nearly a quarter of an hour. As quickly as it had begun, it was over, with the dolphins disappearing en masse as though to a call.

'This episode caused much excitement within the group and was the topic of conversation on the long trip back to Whangamata. It was one of the highlights of our diving careers, and we can't wait for another chance to interlock with these amazing mammals, hopefully for longer next time.'

At midday, Easter, 1988, Bill Clementson, Steve Joyce and Paul Rose were off the Coromandel coast in a runabout.

'We had just decided to go home, when Steve saw bottlenose dolphins near Mahurangi Island. We went over, and I jumped in with my mask, snorkel and fins. I saw a mother and a baby below me, so dived down towards them. Perhaps my dive was too sudden, or Mum was just being protective, because they both did a sharp turn and bolted. A group of four to six other dolphins came in my direction and swam below me. I dived down towards them as they passed. They eyed me but didn't stop to play.

'I got back into the boat, and we followed the dolphins as they headed towards South Sunk Rock and a group of boats fishing there. They started jumping out of the water, almost vertically in some instances, three-quarters out, then falling backwards or sideways as well as forward. Several dolphins—altogether there were about 12 at this stage—started bow-riding off our boat. This bow-riding continued with different dolphins for most of the rest of the encounter. They kept right on the bow of the boat, just under the water. We could lie on the bow of the boat and be less than a metre from them, watching them just under us, with them occasionally looking up at us as well—tremendous!

'The impression I had was that they were interested in us, but when I entered the water I hadn't been mobile enough to keep up with them. However, the boat could match their speed, so I decided to try something different. I tied a length of rope onto the back of the boat and jumped into the water with just mask and snorkel, holding onto the end of the rope. With the boat towing me, I could maintain the speed of the dolphins and had a limited amount of manoeuvrability. By holding out one arm or the other, I was able to swing out to either side, and I could also perform very shallow dives while the boat was dragging me.

'The dolphins stayed with the boat while I was in the water and made several passes close to me, obviously quite interested. It was a fantastic feeling being able to cruise along at their speed, almost as part of the school. Often a young dolphin would swing towards me or the boat, only to veer away again suddenly and return to its mother. It is interesting to speculate whether it was just a case of nerves or whether it was being recalled by an anxious mother.

'After a while I got out, and Paul swapped places with me, as we only had the one mask and snorkel on the boat. Another group of dolphins caught up with us from behind, making a total of about 60 in the combined school. Paul said that he got a good response to his singing into the snorkel while being dragged. I had equally good interactions with the dolphins whether I made sounds or not. I think that the novelty of the situation interested the dolphins more than any sounds we made.

'Steve swapped places with Paul. Since Steve wasn't used to the mask and snorkel, he only wore a mask. This necessitated going slower so that there was less of a "head" wave when he lifted his head out of the water to breathe, so we sped ahead of the dolphins and dropped him off in front of them. He got some really good views of the school swimming past him. While they were passing, one dolphin was swimming upside down just under the surface, parallel to Steve, slowly slapping its tail on the surface over and over again. I responded by slapping a flipper on the surface, but nothing more eventuated from this.

'I got into the water again ahead of the school, with the boat dragging me. As the school caught up with me, they were even more numerous than before, dolphins underwater on both sides. It was really fabulous! At times, I had several dolphins flanking me several metres away on either side. And on one occasion, a single large dolphin came to within half a metre of me on my left-hand side and just swam beside me like that, eye-to-eye. It was really tremendous.'

13: Dolphin Swimming at Kapiti Island

Project Interlock's first report of a lengthy encounter with common dolphins, *Delphinus delphis*, besides our own at the Poor Knights Islands, came from Alan Morrison, who met this shyer species at Kapiti Island, on the west coast near Wellington. Ensuing reports show this to be an important place for meeting common dolphins. Fortunately, it has now been made a Marine Reserve.

In November 1979 Alan and his diving club were planning a dive at the north end of Kapiti.

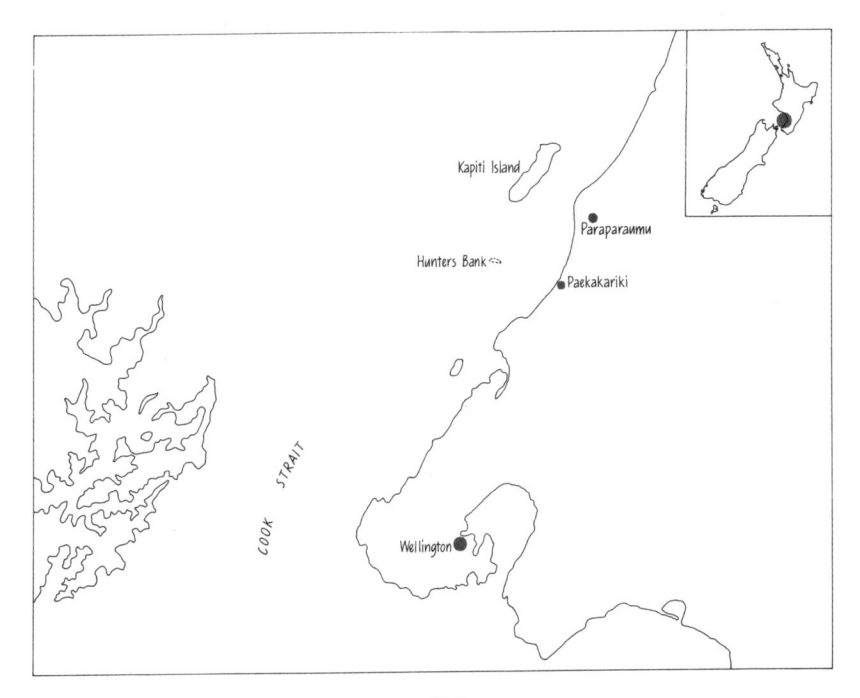

'Shortly after leaving the beach, my girlfriend, Shirley Farthing, spotted dolphins. We headed towards them. I relinquished control of the boat, hurriedly threw my mask and fins on, and hit the water. They were *Delphinus*, and the great thing was that they did not flee. With the boat just idling and drifting, the dolphins were cavorting around. I found if I dolphin-kicked down, they would appear. I swam in tight circles, and they did the same but much faster.

'By this time my companion had entered the water, and the four other boatloads of our divers had converged on us and were entering. With our five boats just about stationary and milling around, and about ten divers in the water, I thought the dolphins would move away, but they didn't. They seemed to delight in dashing from diver to diver.

'My own experiences were that the longer I was under the water the longer contact was continued: the dolphins would streak past and disappear into the gloom, with about 7 metres visibility, only to return from the rear and repeat the manoeuvre. There were about nine dolphins in our area; a much larger group continued following a boat over to the island.

'After about 25 minutes, some of our group continued on their way, and the dolphins followed. I boarded my boat, and away we went on our course. We were almost immediately joined by the dolphins again. They rode our bow wave. I waited till we were ahead of them and entered the water. What followed was another 30 minutes of "games". Again we had four boats and many divers in the water, and still the dolphins stayed.

'At one stage the dolphins appeared to lose interest and began to move away. One of our members was circling in his boat, and they picked up his bow wave. He then returned to where we were still in the water, whereupon the dolphins left him and returned to us. I must stress that at no stage did anyone actually chase them—they could have swum off at any time.

'One particular dolphin was distinctly marked with parallel scars like giant fingernail scratches. Another smaller dolphin appeared to be a bit of a loner from the rest of the group, turning up by himself at intervals. I noticed at one point during our first dive that one of the dolphins appeared to defecate directly in front of a diver.

'When I eventually climbed back into my boat, the dolphins were still in the area. Unfortunately I was exhausted, as were most of the others. All in all, it was one of the best experiences I've had in the sea, and I'm looking forward to meeting those dolphins again.'

The following year, Alan and Shirley had a second meeting out in Cook Strait, near Kapiti Island.

'En route to Hunters Bank, a reef about 8 kilometres south of Kapiti Island, we encountered common dolphins, about 15 of them. They rode our bow wave for perhaps five minutes before departing. We did not linger in the area for long, as we planned to dive Hunters, which must be the area's top spot—only possible at slack tide. However, a solitary dolphin rejoined us from the group and frolicked in front of our boat for about 15 minutes before he veered to the west and left us.

A couple of hours later, after diving Hunters, we were again joined by common dolphins on our return trip in the same area, about 5 kilometres off Paekakariki. They could have been the same group we had seen on our outward journey.

'Slowing the boat down, we rang a small hand bell. I decided to enter the water, and my buddy accompanied me. Shirley Farthing stayed in the boat and rang the bell. I dolphin-kicked down and went through my usual procedure of swimming as fast as I could in circles, which usually prompts the dolphins to do the same. As they alternately surfaced and dived, I would swim down with them as far as I dared. The visibility was excellent, about 20 metres, and I was able to get a good look at them for distinguishing features. One had a torn dorsal fin and some white markings in front of it.

'As I entered the water, one dolphin had defecated, not directly in front of me but at a distance of about 6 metres. Then they came very close, about a metre, often turning slightly to one side so as to bring an eye to bear on us and get a good look. Many had scratches on them, but I could not readily isolate any particular individuals. After about 18 minutes they left, and we returned to the boat.

'We continued on our way for a few hundred metres and were again joined by them or a similar group, which Shirley said had been travelling just behind the main group. We stopped the boat, and Shirley jumped in. The dolphins did a few circuits around her and then moved away. I rang the bell and they came back. They only moved about 50 metres away. As I sat in the boat on a glassy sea, the dolphins came right up to us, very slowly on the surface, their exhalations sounding for all the world like a "slightly puffed" snorkeller returning to the boat. They again turned to bring one eye to bear on us.

'Shirley took the bell, rang it in the water, and spent about 15 minutes frolicking with them before they lost interest and moved off.'

By 1981 the Kapiti Underwater Club had become very enthusiastic about diving with common dolphins. Mid Beckett describes one of his encounters early that year:

'Graham and I spotted a school of dolphins in the channel on our way to Kapiti, and it almost seemed they were waiting for us to appear, as we had contacted dolphins on our previous two trips to Kapiti.

'Although we could not tell if they were in fact the same animals each time, their response on seeing our aluminium catamaran heading their way was unmistakable. They immediately approached us, and when we shut down the outboards they treated us to a truly magnificent display of aquabatics, rushing the boat and leaping clear of the water to smash back in right beside the boat.

'Graham and I quickly donned our gear and, grasping the underwater movie camera, we leapt into the water with the dolphins to enjoy the most enviable experience of our lives. The dolphins would cruise around on the perimeter of our vision, then race madly towards us, and at the last moment would execute a perfect barrel roll or leap to shoot past us at breathtaking speed.

'At one stage towards the end of the encounter, Graham and I were close to the surface, approximately 2 metres apart, when a particularly friendly dolphin approached. This fellow gave us a very careful examination while swimming slowly around us. Then he suddenly turned and, with a comical, almost human-like gesture of laughter, raced straight towards us and shot with dazzling beauty of motion between us, within a metre of us both.

'We were so thrilled with this obvious demonstration of friendliness that we felt we could have stayed with them forever, but shortly afterwards these lovely animals bid us farewell and left us to clamber back into the boat—tired but elated.'

Within a few weeks of this encounter, Mike Young met about 25 common dolphins off the northern end of Kapiti. When first noticed, they were not playing and showed no interest in his runabout. What ensued was a most unusual and deliberate demonstration of dolphin love making—virtually a communication to the divers!

'We approached cautiously. Bruce and I donned snorkels and slipped very quietly over the side to try to initiate contact. We quickly discovered that the common dolphins did not appreciate our joining them in the water, and they moved away some 60–100 metres and continued to mill quietly in a group.

'After ten minutes, we rejoined the boat and decided that I would gear up for scuba while Bruce would stay on snorkel to see if this resulted in more confidence on the part of the dolphins. We moved very slowly over to the school and both slipped quietly into the water once more.

'The change in the dolphins' attitude this time was quite marked, for as I drifted down to about 20 metres I could see the school quite clearly about 20 metres away, and having noticed me they peeled off in groups of four or five to come and investigate. I was quite excited at this new experience and spent the next 15 minutes rising slowly back to about 10 metres, then sinking down again to 20 metres, and so on. The dolphins came rushing straight for me in groups of five or six, taking a good look as they cruised around me within 2 metres, and rising towards Bruce, on snorkel, circling him before moving well away from both of us to surface for a blow and a breath. This action of going away some distance from us to breathe is quite significant, I feel. It would have been much easier for them to surface near Bruce, as he was already there.

'However, I digress from the most important aspect of the whole encounter. The second or third time the dolphins moved around me, I suddenly noticed that the groups I took to be five to six strong in separate parties, were in fact *groups of pairs*, consisting of up to three pairs, and they were swimming rapidly and constantly belly to belly.

'This was an exceptionally exciting discovery, and I carefully watched the next approaching group. Lo and behold, they certainly *were* together and they certainly *were* mating. I could very clearly and distinctly see the sexual contact, and in several instances could actually see the male's penis thrusting and retracting as the pair circled me 1–3 metres away. These animals would, after completing a circuit of me, separate and shoot back up towards Bruce, and in several instances would recommence copulation while circling around him. He was also consequently able to observe this act in some detail.

'Unfortunately I was so excited at this turn of events that I am uncertain of whether they were changing partners or not, especially as the five-to-six strong groups were taking turns in successively contacting me, and I failed to specifically watch any particular couple. I must say that I have the definite impression that they were in fact changing partners during this contact. I tried various kicks and barrel rolls in the water, but I feel in this situation contact in the water on scuba was much better maintained while I simply remained passive and allowed the action to occur around me. The only factor of real note is that the dolphins did not seem to mind Bruce on snorkel while I was below him on scuba, but they definitely avoided contact while we were *both* on snorkel.

'They definitely showed a preference for my company for continuous contact, but they also maintained sporadic contact with Bruce at the same time.'

Project Interlock Reply

'I quite agree that your quiet, passive role was most appropriate under the circumstances, which were unusual. I think the less communicative response of the dolphins was probably related to their mating ritual. Perhaps their entire behaviour was being directed towards you! The body language, frolics, barrel rolls, various kicks, etc. is only appropriate when we meet dolphins who are frolicsome in their approach to us. Fortunately you sensed this was not so, and the passive approach enabled you to observe something rarely witnessed at such a close range.'

Encounters in the Kapiti area intensified in 1984–85. David and Leon Williams sent us many reports.

'The common dolphins we met on Christmas Day 1984 were in a fairly large group of 20 or more, which contained only one or two young. There were two of us in the water at one time. They seemed to come

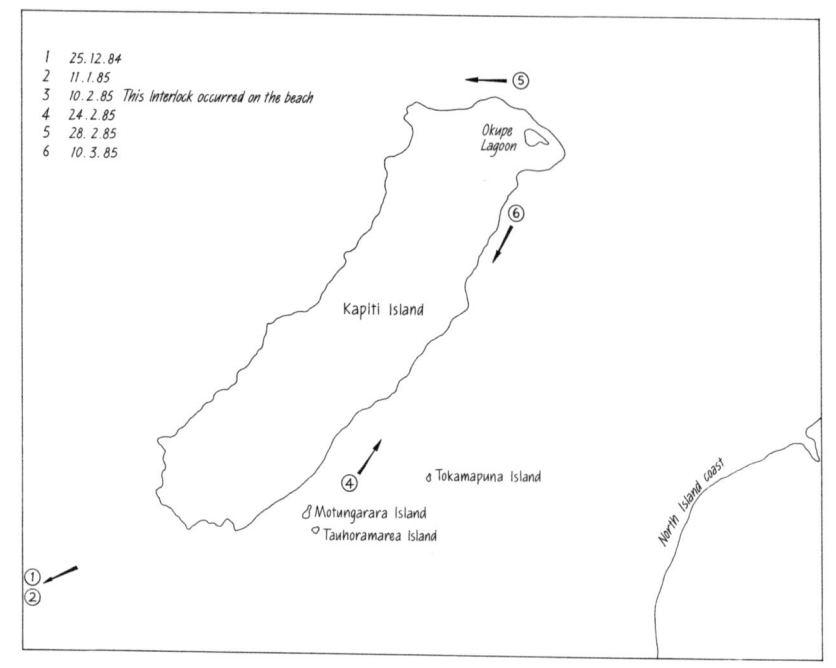

1	25.12.84
2	11.1.85
3	10.2.85 This interlock occurred on the beach
4	24.2.85
5	28.2.85
6	10.3.85

Okupe Lagoon

Kapiti Island

Tokamapuna Island
Motungarara Island
Tauhoramarea Island

North Island coast

extremely close. At times they filled our field of vision, approaching well within touching distance, though they didn't stop moving. We were in the water for at least 45 minutes, never losing sight of at least one dolphin. The boat remained stationary.

'They were more attracted to us when we were doing the dolphin-kick than the normal kick. There were feeding birds in the area, small birds, grey and brown in colour, but they had been feeding in the area all summer. We were in deep water about a kilometre off the southeast corner of Kapiti. The sea was fairly choppy with a northerly wind. We were the only boat out at this time, 11 a.m.

'Since this encounter, we have had two more dives with dolphins, all on snorkel. The second was totally different from the first.

'There were no feeding birds at all: the group only contained about ten, one-third being young. As soon as my brother and friend entered the water they disappeared, surfacing some distance away.

'We made three attempts before finally giving up; they carried on northwards. This occurred about midday, with a calm sea, on 11 January 1985.

'The third encounter was much the same as the first, but again, there were no birds. This was on 10 February 1985. We found a group of 15 or more 2 kilometres off Paraparaumu beach. When we stopped the boat, they seemed to halt in the water as if waiting for me to get in.'

14: Dolphins & Swimmers in Cook Strait

One day a friend sent us a news clipping from the Wellington *Evening Post*, dated 3 April 1978, showing a girl in mid-ocean surrounded by dolphin fins. It is an interesting comment on the low general level of dolphin knowledge that the newspaper had not stressed the uniqueness of the photo, even though such encounters are rare.

I had a hunch there was more to this story, and wrote to the girl, 16-year-old long-distance swimmer Meda McKenzie. Her name was already familiar to us for her exploits. Meda was the first person to thoroughly conquer the powerful currents of Cook Strait, by swimming the windy gap between the two main islands from both north and south.

She has swum the English Channel, the Bristol Channel and, grimmest of all, the chill southern waters of Foveaux Strait.

Maori tradition surrounding the famous Cook Strait dolphin Pelorus

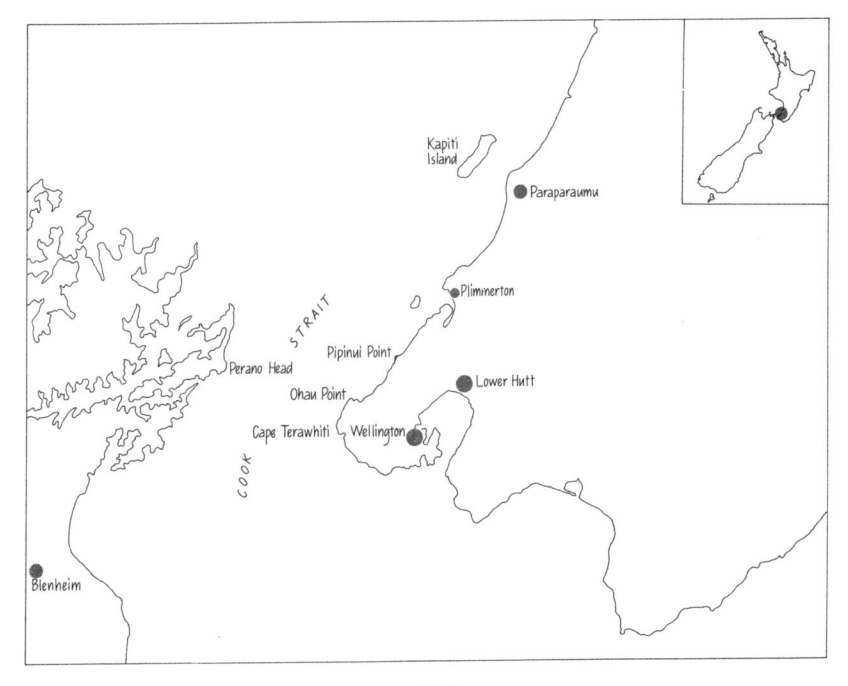

Jack (1888–1912) tells of Hinepoupou, who was marooned by her husband on Kapiti Island and swam Cook Strait to her South Island home, aided by a dolphin she called to assist her.

In his book *The Perano Whalers* John Grady describes the exploits of earlier Cook Strait swimmers who were boat-escorted by the famous Perano family, the whalers of Picton. From the failed attempts of Lily Copplestone (1929), Bill Penny and Margaret Sweeney (both 1962) until Barry Davenport's success that same year, there are no references to dolphins. But Bill Penny, on his 1 March 1962 swim, had to abandon the water within 3.21 kilometres of Ohau Point and success—because of sharks. Escort vessels even carried sharp-shooters . . .

The fishermen of Island Bay, Wellington, fondly called Meda their 'dolphin girl'. The news photo showed her swimming from Kapiti to the mainland. Her story could just as easily become a legend.

To us she wrote:

'I hope my answer to your letter is not too late. I have had a number of encounters with the dolphins, and I feel a certain kinship with them, as they always appear when I am in Cook Strait and I am quite sure that they come to protect me, especially when I am swimming in the dark, as I can hear them calling long before they reach me. When a swim is abandoned, they don't leave until just beforehand, and each time one dolphin has surfaced right beside me, flipped in front of me and back again, as if to say, "Don't go on."

'This is quite different from my successful swims, when they have frolicked beside me and been very playful, as if they knew the tides and weather were going to hold.

'On the Kapiti swim it was very rough, and a strong rip was running about a kilometre off the island. A school of dolphins appeared, and one mother and baby came up beside me; the adult or mother swam beside me, but the baby swam in front and kept flipping over and coming up so that it brushed across my face almost as though trying to kiss me. It would then swim a few metres in front of me and sort of waggle its tail, then look back, and I'm quite sure the look said, "Come on, you can do it. Follow me." They stayed till about 400 metres offshore. Then they circled me, joined the rest of the dolphins, and swam off out to sea.

'I know when dolphins are playing and when they are serious. I guess you do too. With me, if there is danger ahead, they time my arm movements, and when my hand goes into the water to start my pull through they nip it away so that I can't swim. If they are playing, they then dive under me and come up when the next arm pull is ready. If they are serious they stay right beside me and make a funny noise, almost warning me that I can go no further.'

On receiving this I sent Meda a list of questions on her dolphin encounters, and from her replies learnt as follows:

On her first Cook Strait swim, from north to south (3 February 1978), Meda met dolphins 5 kilometres out, after leaving Ohau Point at 10 a.m. Three kilometres off Perano Head, on the other side of Cook Strait, they left. She set foot on the South Island at 10 p.m., after swimming 28.4 kilometres in 12 hours 7 minutes.

Her second Cook Strait crossing, from south to north, took place two weeks later, 17 February 1978. Meda set out near Perano Head at 2 p.m. Six kilometres out she met dolphins, who stayed with her to within 3 kilometres of her landing at Pipinui Point an hour before midnight.

That April, on an easier training swim from Kapiti Island to Paraparaumu Beach, Meda met the dolphins a kilometre offshore, and they escorted her to close to the beach. Next year Meda tried the Cook Strait crossing twice more to improve her times. Both these swims had to be abandoned because of weather conditions. On the first attempt (14 February 1979) dolphins arrived when she was 5 kilometres from Pipinui Point and stayed with her until she left the water after four hours' effort. On her second attempt a week later (20 February 1979) dolphins arrived when she was 6 kilometres out. At seven that evening deteriorating weather forced her out.

'While I was in the shower, the pilot and my father said one dolphin kept skidding on its tail and calling. It came right up to the boat. Fifteen minutes after my leaving the water, the fog cleared and the wind dropped. I could have kept going . . .'

Meda believes the dolphins to be both *Tursiops* and *Delphinus*. 'The small ones come very close, swimming round, under and beside me. I'm sure they think I'm one of them.' I wondered whether the dolphins might simply be riding the bow of the boat, but Meda allayed this doubt:

'The distance between the boat and the dolphins varies from 10 metres to half a kilometre, while with me they are from half a metre to mere centimetres!'

Wearing goggles, she was able to watch their antics but hadn't learnt to recognise individuals, though she had a hunch: 'One at least has come to me more than once. I don't know why I know. I just sort of feel it.'

On other long-distance swims elsewhere in New Zealand and Europe she had never encountered dolphins. While it seems incredible, the behaviour of the dolphins suggested to Meda they were aware of her capacity and what she was attempting to do. She definitely felt a great assistance in having them by her side.

Finally Meda wrote, 'I am starting scuba lessons and hope to come north this summer. I would love to come out with you and Jan to see if my dolphins only look after me in Cook Strait or if dolphins in other places will come to me.' Meda's wish was to come true . . .

Near dusk on 24 March 1980, 18-year-old Belinda Shields crawled ashore on hands and knees at Cape Terawhiti, the tip of the North Island, after swimming Cook Strait in 8 hours 32 minutes. About one hour after leaving the South Island a group of 60 common dolphins had joined her.

'I heard them coming—strange underwater noises that got very loud. I realised they would probably be dolphins, as I'd seen a school of them beside the launch the day before when we crossed to the South Island.

'They came very close and actually rubbed against me, underneath and alongside. It scared me a little, as I had no previous experience of dolphins, but I knew as long as they were there I had no fear of sharks. It seemed they actually wanted me to play—very excited, jumping out of the water and chattering between themselves. It certainly broke the boredom for me.

'Prior to their arrival I was feeling a bit disillusioned with the cold water—between 10 and 13° Celsius. It gave me a splitting headache. The sea was rough and the sky very dark. I was uncertain of making the swim, let alone breaking the record. When the dolphins came, it took my mind off the cold, and I was excited to have these beautiful creatures swim with me. I watched their behaviour, and it pumped my spirits up. I'm not sure if there were any babies with them, but they came in many sizes, so perhaps there were. After about two hours they disappeared, only to return half an hour later. Again I heard them coming—it was very loud underwater. They still seemed very excited and stayed with me until within 5 kilometres of the North Island.'

On this crossing Meda McKenzie was on board the launch and paced the swimmer towards the end.

On her honeymoon Meda and her husband, John Sweetman, came to Northland. At 8 a.m. on 15 December 1979, Meda swam from the Tutukaka coast out to the Poor Knights Islands, a distance of 19 kilometres. Her main worry was that the warmth of the water might make her go to sleep. She reached the island near Rikoriko Cave at 4.27 p.m.

Five kilometres from the mainland common dolphins had appeared. Following the swimmer with our catamaran, Jan and I were surprised. Almost every day for the week before the swim we had been to sea and sighted no dolphins in the area. For a week afterwards we were out frequently and still saw none. Yet there they were, after Meda had been swimming offshore for 90 minutes.

It was a weird day for a long-distance swim. A 30-knot offshore breeze nearly put a stop to it, but Meda was determined to try. Her original intention was to swim from the islands to the shore, but sea conditions ruled that out.

The moment we put the catamaran's noses out of Tutukaka Harbour we learnt that there would be no need of sail or engine. With *Interlock* supporters Joyce and Graham Adams to assist us, for once Jan and I broke our rule about not going to sea when winds greater than 20 knots were forecast. We found ourselves moving at nearly 3 knots with a bare pole and were obliged to tack to and fro to keep pace with Meda.

Just ahead of the swimmer, two men, her father and coach, huddled in our inflatable, giving her encouragement and keeping her on course. The mother ship, a 40-foot motor vessel, *Geisha*, hovered nearby.

This dolphin girl hardly used her legs, just hauling herself through the following seas with powerful armstrokes. Our hearts went out to her, so tiny and alone in all that wild ocean. With CB radio we were linked to another long-distance swimming event some 400 kilometres south, where eight people were racing from Whakatane out to Whale Island and back to shore, right through the area of Ramari ('Dusty') Stewart's Interlock II dolphin study. We wondered if those swimmers would encounter dolphins too.

It was 9.30 when we noticed dolphins about 200 metres away heading south towards the coast, as if going right past us. Jan called to them. She knew their presence would help Meda enormously if she were to keep going in such hectic conditions. To our delight the dolphins slowed and milled around before turning directly towards us, their fins slicing the waves. Jan and I were hugging each other with joy when they surfaced alongside Meda. There were six: four on one side and a pair just ahead.

Meda saw a baby dolphin flanked by its mother and an 'auntie'. The mother was closest to her. They then circled, playing around for several minutes before being lost to our view in the whitecaps. Twice more on her journey dolphins appeared around the swimmer briefly, as if checking her out. Meda was ploughing along strongly when, only a kilometre from the steep cliffs a fierce squall swept her away to the north. With utter tenacity she just kept on stroking. She seemed to claw her way to her goal.

On the long hard slog home we really learnt the wind's strength. With power and sail it took us six hours—not much less than Meda's 8 hours 27 minutes. Twice (at 5.10 and 6.27 p.m.) we were visited by the same small group of common dolphins. Their company made us feel a lot less lonely.

Following the progress of the Whakatane offshore race, we discovered no dolphins were sighted by the swimmers down there, although they were in the vicinity (see page 116).

In November 1981 Belinda Shields, Phillip Rush and Elizabeth Horner made a relay swim from Great Barrier Island to Takapuna Beach. During the night, Elizabeth was surrounded by a dozen dolphins, swooping around her, chattering and even touching her. All tiredness vanished. She tried talking to them and believed she heard answers. When it was Belinda's turn she felt they were deliberately assisting her. But Phillip, never having met dolphins before, felt a certain unease. They left when he entered, but returned five minutes later.

The Cook Strait saga evolved further when Donna Bouzaid made an attempt on 1 May 1985. Donna, 22, was the thirty-third to succeed, and her time, eight and a quarter hours, was the fastest north-south swim by a woman.

At nine in the morning, with a quarter of the distance to go, Donna was battling towards the South Island, fighting fatigue and cold, the sheer purgatory that marathon swimmers endure, when seven common dolphins surrounded her, whistling and frolicking.

'Seeing them spurred me on. My swim goggles made it very clear. They were so playful, chasing each other and doing somersaults. Twice I ducked under and watched them. I was surprised that I didn't scare them off. One of the smaller dolphins actually clipped across me and slightly flicked my goggles. Others swam right next to me and close beneath.'

For one and a half hours the dolphins stayed with her. Donna had never made a long ocean swim before and felt the dolphins had arrived at just the right time.

On 18 March 1982 Cook Strait dolphins again hit the headlines: 'Dolphins Help Swimmers'. For the first time Australian and New Zealand relay teams had competed to cross the Strait. The 53-kilometre swim from Perano Head to Plimmerton was won by the Australians in 8 hours 14 minutes—but they believed they had been favoured by dolphin escorts.

Australian team captain John Koorey said that the dolphins latched on to his team and chased off a 4-metre shark that was showing too much interest in the race. This episode was captured by a television news camera. John felt sure that the presence of the dolphins had eased his agony in the water.

'I had ten of them swimming around me. I've never experienced anything like it. The dolphins were making these noises, and it sounded to us as if they were saying, "Come on, Aussies. Come on." There were four in front of me and three on each side. They really helped take my mind off the pain I was in. After about an hour the dolphins disappeared—for a while. Later I learnt there had been a 4-metre shark hanging around. The dolphins had sent him off before coming back to join me.'

On 10 February 1988, Phillip Rush attempted the first triple crossing of Cook Strait. A front-page *Dominion* newspaper photograph shows Phillip pausing for a drink with a dolphin close by. On his third leg sea conditions conquered him—but he no longer had the least fear of dolphins.

15: Dolphin Swimming in the Marlborough Sounds

The Marlborough Sounds offer the unusual opportunity to meet four species of dolphins within its vast array of waterways.

This account by Christchurch fisheries scientist Malcolm Flain is of special interest, as it suggests two groups of bottlenose dolphins may have communicated at long range about their meeting with a strange diving mammal. It is also one of the earliest on record—yet Malcolm showed no fear . . .

'It all happened because of a difference in attitude to our holiday. There were four of us and two boats; we were staying at Richmond Bay on Kenny Island in the Pelorus Sound in February 1974.

'Two of us were tired of getting up before dawn to go fishing, so on this day we slept in while the other pair went off early. The arrangement was that we would start out later, do some fishing on our own, then meet

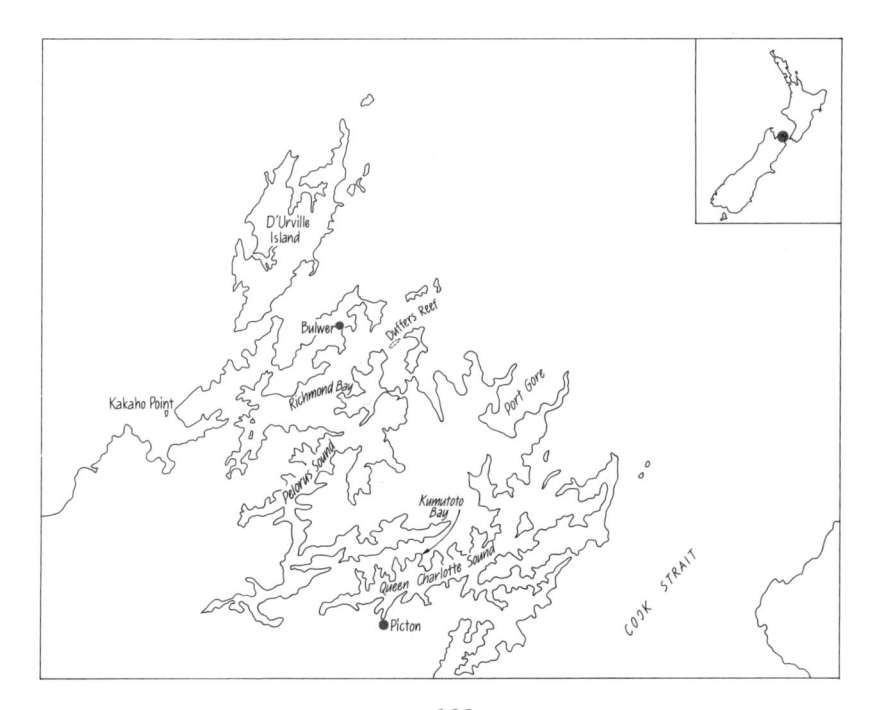

133

up at west entry point and bring the other pair *their* breakfast!

'Later, when we got there, there was no sign of them, so we did our fishing and I did some snorkelling for the dinner table. Eventually we grew impatient with waiting and moved offshore to be able to see further and be seen.

'It worked. Away in the distance we saw the other boat, but it was moving rapidly away from us. We gave chase, and as we got closer we initially thought that they were playing a very large fish, but as we drew alongside, out in the centre of the Kakaho Channel, we saw that they had been keeping company with a school of bottlenose dolphins.

'When the boats stopped, so did the dolphins, circling us and clearly curious. I grabbed my mask and snorkel and was in. The dolphins immediately started circling me, echo-locating with clicks and communicating with squeaks. There were 16 large adults. I was completely fascinated. The water was very clear and they were very curious.

'Meanwhile, back on the surface, and unknown to me, my friends saw, way out from the open sea, a very large school of dolphins speeding towards the boats, leaping as they came. They had evidently been called up to see the weird human animals by the dolphins circling me.

'The first thing I knew about it was that suddenly I was surrounded by a wall of dolphins, mostly adults and very large. Like the others, they circled me, on occasions no further away from me than an arm's length. I was regularly snorkelling down to about 10 metres, at which time I had them all around me, above and below. Mums were bringing their babies to get a good view, clearly eyeballing me at no distance, and I was revelling in the experience. At one stage I thought I was hallucinating, because suddenly I saw birds, glistening with trapped air, flying past me at 10 metres. These turned out to be Cape pigeons, no doubt attracted by the goings-on. I tried to count the dolphins, and gave up at 64. My friends on top estimated 150–200.

'Eventually, after 20 minutes, the dolphins had seen enough; it was noticeable that they circled further away, with thinning ranks, and then they were gone except for their sounds.

'I hadn't had nearly enough, so I climbed back into the boat and we caught up with a small group so that I could jump in again. At first there was no sign of them, then half a dozen appeared briefly, circled me a few times, and then veered off. That was the end of one of my most memorable dives ever. I still retain the experience of a once-in-a-lifetime encounter with hundreds of dolphins.'

At Port Gore in the Marlborough Sound, John Montgomery had an encounter with the tiny Hector's dolphins in May 1981. This was the first diver contact with them on our file. We have many reports of surfers meeting Hector's dolphins all around the South Island, especially at

Kaikoura, Akaroa, Waikawa and Buller River, and as far north as the Kawhia and Manukau Harbours and Piha. John had already dived with bottlenose and common dolphins in the North Island.

'They showed no interest in the boat, so I just jumped overboard in the middle of them. They located me in the water, even though the visibility was only 5–7 metres, with no difficulty. The reason I mention this is because, unlike common and bottlenose, they made not a single sound —in fact it was rather eerie. I would assume that they do communicate but have an inaudible frequency. I had the same two animals swimming with me for about 30 minutes of the interlock. The only problem was that I could not keep up. They solved this by coming back for me. I had very close contact with these two. At no time did I try to touch either of them, and they stayed within my reach, one on each side of me, doing barrel rolls and mimicking me—or was it me mimicking them?

'The only problem is that I can't snorkel as well as dolphins, which annoys me at times, especially when they came within centimetres of me.

'Contact was broken after about 40 minutes by mutual departure.'

Around this time Colin Pearce met dusky dolphins in Pelorus Sound, on the north side of Duffers Reef. His diving group was aboard Ken Gullery's charter boat *Glenmore*.

'The two dusky dolphins were first seen bow-hopping under our boat. The skipper asked if we wanted to get in with them, and of course we jumped at the chance. Three snorkellers were into their suits and over the side within a minute. The dolphins were very active, darting and diving around us for the whole 30 minutes we were in the water. They seemed to like me turning, diving and rolling, as they would follow me in whatever I would do. When they swam away, I would call out "Here dolphins" or something similar, and they would nearly always swim back towards me. One of my buddies blew on his whistle underwater, and this also seemed to attract them.

'They stayed near us for about 30 minutes, then disappeared completely—bored I guess.

'The sea was dead flat at the time, with visibility of about 6 metres. The dolphins didn't have any unusual markings and appeared to be in very good condition, 2 metres long. They came within about a metre of us. Ken Gullery said that was the closest he'd seen them come.

'As all three divers were keen underwater hockey players, we were using dolphin-kick: this may have helped to keep them interested.

'This is my second interlock experience; the first was about a year ago with eight duskies. They were feeding near the Chetwodes and weren't quite so interested in the two divers in the water. They only stayed around for about ten minutes.'

On New Year's Day 1982 Craig Potton met bottlenose dolphins in Pelorus Sound.

'At nine in the morning I noticed dolphins swimming and jumping close to shore at Tuna Bay, a very long way up Pelorus Sound from the open sea. My brother, his girlfriend and I jumped into an aluminium dinghy with a small outboard and zoomed across to where they were. I jumped in with them but in my excitement had forgotten my snorkel. They swam towards me and under me, often in groups of three, and making a lot of noise. Many came across to investigate—changing course towards me on the surface till about 10 metres away, then diving 2 metres below me while passing beneath—a few passed beside. I stayed with them in the water for 15 minutes, but although I loved watching them I felt a bit silly being unable to dive or swim effectively without snorkel or weights. But I loved the experience and shouted at them underwater.

'Then we drove the boat alongside them and they really responded. There were probably 150 in the bay around us—big healthy bottlenose, with few fin marks compared to our Nelson group, and they would come from quite some distance to check us out. We were whistling really loud, tapping the side of the hull in various rhythms, and dangling our hands and feet over the bow. There were other boats around, but no-one else was responding to them—in fact the other boaties just stopped and watched the dolphins pass them by after cursory visits.

'Again they tended to come in threes under the boat, and some were up to 4 metres long. Their pressure waves lifted our dinghy in the air at times. It was utterly marvellous—they would lie on their sides while swimming flat out, probably at about 30 kilometres per hour, and listening to us.

'I'm sure they preferred the whistling to the hull tapping and, like my lousy swimming, I also felt our music was pretty inadequate. One that continually came under the boat was pregnant, I would say. She had a huge stomach. Their general direction was northwards, but if you drove at them they would turn and swim south, playing with us for a kilometre, then returning again. Occasionally we would slow down or stop, and they would slowly cruise by, but they preferred our top speed and sometimes would stream ahead of the boat and leap into the air. They'd even let us touch their tails over the front of the boat. One near the shore spent time with its tail in the air flapping while moving very slowly.'

Then Judith Winter met dolphins on her way back to Bulwer after a day's fishing. She was so eager to dive with them, she almost leapt in without her gear.

'The three of us jumped in and were immediately surrounded by dolphins—about a dozen. I was particularly struck by the passage in your book about the dolphins defecating directly in front of divers, because that is exactly what we all commented on when we returned to the boat. While we never touched the dolphins, we were within a hand's breadth of them on several occasions. One dolphin was extremely friendly, a big one, and we all assumed he was a male, for some reason. He had two cuts below his left eye and stayed the closest, and would swim around us in tight circles until we were giddy. We stayed in the water with them for about 25 minutes and all felt a great empathy with them—I can't wait for the next time!'

On a calm, sunny winter's day in July 1985, Margaret Stone was returning from a fishing trip. As their launch motored into Kumoto Bay, they saw dolphins milling around a yacht.

'Fortunately we were already in our wetsuits, so Brian and I quickly grabbed our snorkelling gear and swam over to the main group of dolphins. Initially I was rather apprehensive, but having read interlock articles, I had wanted to do this for some time, and until now the opportunity had never presented itself.

'What an experience! Those lovely creatures swimming right up underneath us: I felt I could touch them as they passed underneath, but on trying to, I found that they were still a little distance off. I would hear their whistles, then they'd appear from the murk. The visibility was around 7 metres, which meant we'd hear them coming before sighting them. They appeared to roll onto their sides to watch us as they passed by. Sometimes it would be just one; other times two or three together coming close. I used the dolphin-kick mostly, as I had read that this was preferable when swimming or diving among dolphins. When they disappeared, I'd look around on the surface, fearful that they would just go away, but my excited children on the boat would tell us where they were surfacing and when they were coming our way again. We spent 30 minutes with them before they began to move out into the sound following a yacht.

'It was probably just as well, as I was feeling rather tired by then, more from the excitement than anything else, I think. What an experience—one I hope to repeat many times when the opportunity is there.'

16: Swimming with Dolphins at Kaikoura

In 1981 Project Interlock received its first report of divers swimming with dusky dolphins at Kaikoura. This account is especially historic, as over the ensuing years the human/dusky relationship has developed to the point where Kaikoura now has one of the most advanced dolphin swimming situations in the world. Right from the start, the duskies demonstrated their seaweed game.

On 5 April, out from Kaikoura, Jill Smith, Barry Hoskins and Barry Patterson had one and a half hours of fun with a group of duskies. It was a calm day, around 1 p.m., when they sighted dolphins about 4 kilometres offshore and approached with their 4-metre aluminium boat. Eight dolphins swam around the boat showing interest, so Jill rowed while the two men began to snorkel with them. Visibility was 7 metres. Two more duskies joined in but remained separate from each other.

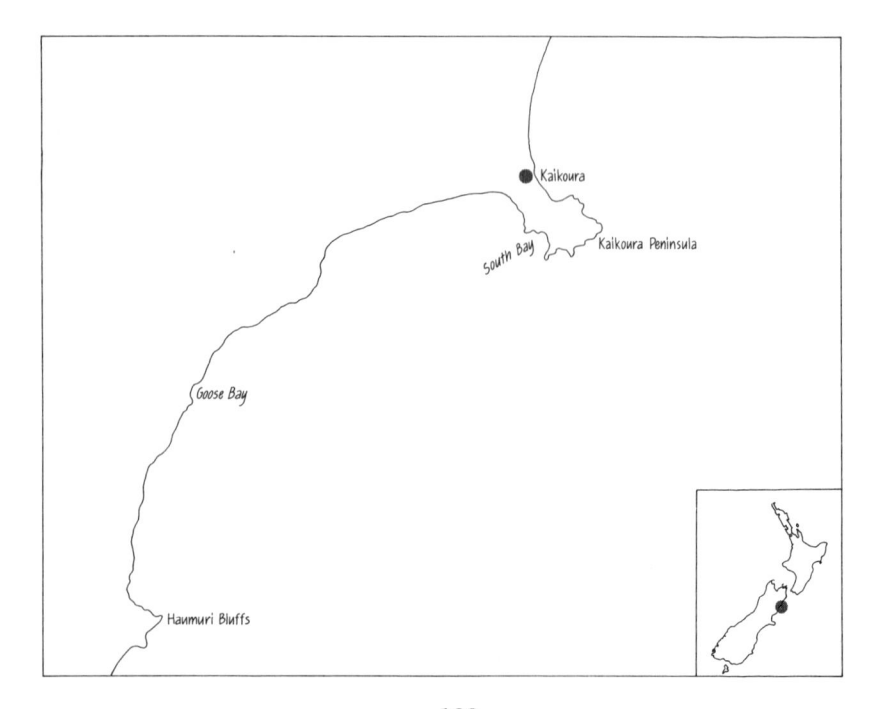

Jill noted. 'Whenever the divers were down, the dolphins seem to surface much more quickly as though in a hurry to get down again. Dolphins often circled them when underwater, and if the divers rotated, the dolphins kept going around until the men felt dizzy. One had the left lobe of its tail fin missing. After three-quarters of an hour we decided to rush back to shore and get a camera. For several hundred metres the dolphins raced alongside, and then they left.

'Half an hour later we returned and found our friends again within five minutes. We took careful note of marks and scars and were able to establish that four dolphins, B, C, D and E, paid particular attention to one diver, while two, A and F, specialised in the other. This time the initial group of eight showed the most interest. The men noted that the dolphins came much closer to them while underwater than on the surface, and both were able to touch dolphins while below.

'There was a game in progress: one had a piece of seaweed draped around its dorsal fin or beak, and there were two in hot pursuit, as if intent on getting the weed. While below, the dolphins would approach the divers head on and veer off at the last minute. The second session lasted about three-quarters of an hour before the divers became fatigued.

'As they left, the dolphins again raced alongside. Then two made a dual leap from the water and all were gone. The divers had often seen dolphins moving along the Kaikoura coastline in large numbers, but sea conditions had not been favourable for joining them.'

In January 1982 Roger Rawling was able to observe duskies mating at Kaikoura. There was a pod of about 200 dolphins, with small groups of seven or eight members swimming on the outskirts.

'There were five dolphins in the group—two were swimming very close, while the remaining three kept their distance. All of a sudden the male dolphin rolled over onto his back and began swimming upside down. He then came up under the female, and for a moment they became locked together with their pectoral fins while their running speed slowed down. After about 15 seconds they parted. This was then repeated three times. All this time the other dolphins kept their distance.'

While filming dusky dolphins off Kaikoura in 1989, 'Wild South' cameraman Andrew Penniket documented the seaweed game perfectly. But he yearned for a diving companion to film, because, as the game developed, he had to become a participant.

Initially we see a dolphin passing the camera hook a scrap of weed on its dorsal fin, surface for a breath, and circle Andrew so closely, we notice a distinct nick in the trailing edge of its dorsal. Then Nickfin surfaces again and circles playfully as a group of companions close in, vying for the weed. Nickfin breathes excitedly, three times in succession, and then swims past the camera again. Directly in front of Andrew it shudders, deliberately flicking the weed off its fin. A challenge!

Another dusky swims up and scoops the weed over its right pectoral, parading it past the camera. And then a third dolphin, this time with a perfect dorsal—Clearfin—passes with the weed hooked on its dorsal. Clearfin releases the weed right in front of the lens. Andrew just has to overcome his detached professional role, reach out for the weed, and toss it out to the dolphins. And so the game continued.

An essential ingredient seems to be the variation of carrying position: fins, tail, beak. It isn't a contest. There doesn't seem to be any snatching: release seems to be voluntary. The exuberant skill needed to catch the weed while rapidly manoeuvring is rather like a non-competitive beach ball game in which humans delight in cooperating to keep the ball in the air.

When humans instigated this game with spotted dolphins in the Bahamas, introducing a T-shirt in lieu of weed, one dolphin eventually vanished with the shirt!

17: Swimming with Dolphins in the Deep South

South of Kaikoura, encounters with dolphins occur, but, for the most part, have not been as intensive or prolonged, for some reason. Project Interlock has reports from as far south as Foveaux Strait.

In February 1981 two paua divers towing an inflatable met a group of 30 bottlenose near Bird Island out from Bluff Harbour. For 30 minutes they dived together, the dolphins approaching the snorkellers within 2 metres. But the tide was taking the men offshore and they had to withdraw*.

At Porpoise Bay in the Catlin Hills near Waikawa Harbour on the

---

* At Bluff Harbour the following year, on almost the same February day, a large solo dolphin turned up at a birdman carnival and joined in the fun with aerial leaps amid temporarily airborne humans.

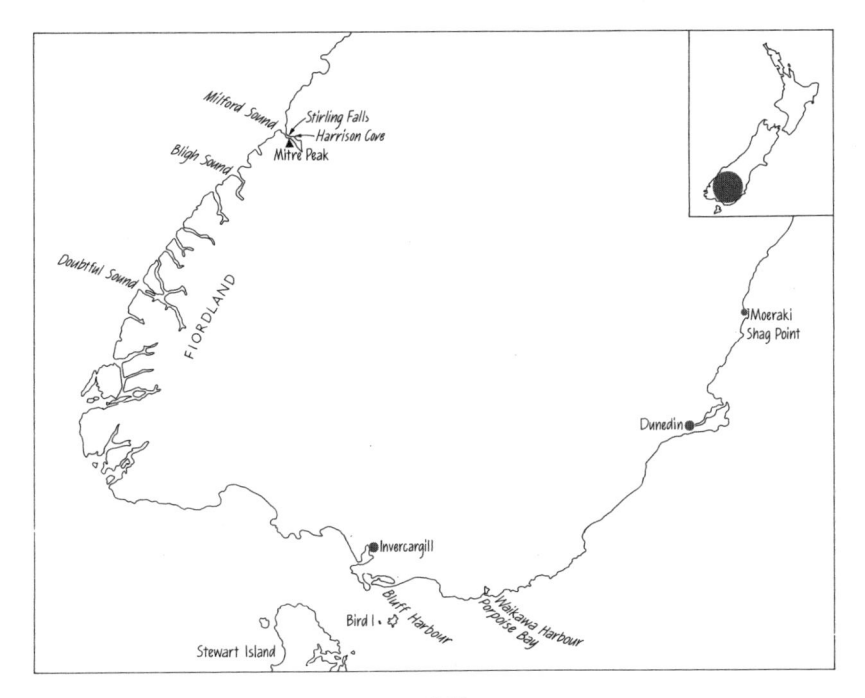

southern coast of Southland, there is a very special place for meeting a group of exceptionally friendly Hector's dolphins. From Labour Weekend to Easter, these tiny cetaceans move inshore to breed and rear their young, in groups of 2–12.

When swimmers approach them in Porpoise Bay, the Hector's dolphins often come into the shallows to investigate, according to Tim Higham: 'darting around our legs, but never close enough to touch. Catching waves is a favourite pastime. I have body-surfed with three dolphins around me, their light-grey bodies and white underbellies glistening in the sun.'

At times these dolphins get so enthusiastic at surfing with humans, or perhaps so reliant on their assistance, that they let themselves get cast ashore by a wave, to be picked up and refloated by their terrestrial companions.

One of the most dramatic encounters in the south was with a solitary bottlenose near Moeraki, north of Dunedin.

In March 1981 Pat Winders found it circling his boat and joined it with snorkel gear. Visibility was around 7 metres.

'The dolphin swam past just beyond my touch, looking me over. He played around me for about 30 minutes. When I clapped my hands, he kicked away and did rolling movements but did not seem frightened. Barry entered the water with scuba. I geared up too. The dolphin came up to him, staying almost still in the water, then moved slowly away and swam lazily about the boat.

'At 11 a.m. we descended the anchor line in search of crays. The bottom was about 15 metres below. At the sand we started our way along the drop-off. Next thing the dolphin was there, suspended tail upmost, head nearly on the sand, and remaining motionless for several seconds at a time. He did this repeatedly.

'At one stage I was poking around in a crevice when I had a feeling I was being watched. I looked around to find the dolphin's head about half a metre away from mine, as if he was trying to see what I was looking at.

'We surfaced at 11.55 and he was still with us. The dolphin then rode our bow and played around the boat for the full half-hour journey back to the bay, coming alongside the boat many times, rolling on his side and playing around.

'He followed us through the channel right into the surf, where the depth was only about a metre. The dolphin had many marks over its entire body, even on the flukes of its tail. They looked like he had been in a net at some stage. The marks were not definite cuts but more like abrasion marks. The encounter was at Rolys Reef, which is between Moeraki and Shag Point.'

In Fiordland bottlenose dolphins are resident in most of the fiords. Encounters have been reported between small groups and scuba-divers in Doubtful Sound (where a population of some 60 has been studied), Bligh Sound and Milford Sound, but as yet without much complexity or duration: usually around ten minutes. Perhaps, in those cold waters, where divers wear thick suits and heavy weights, they have not been very playful. On scuba it is all too easy to remain a passive admirer of dolphins, which for them is not particularly interesting.

But Fiordland dolphins have responded intensively to humans in a different situation: kayakers have had incredible experiences.

One fine frosty July morning in 1990, Ian Daniel and his friends drove over to Milford Sound. Conditions for a kayak cruise were perfect: glassy water, fresh snow on the peaks, and hardly any noisy tourist planes to spoil the tranquility.

'After a pleasant cruise up to the Stirling Falls and back, we pulled into Harrison Cove to stretch our legs and have a late lunch. As we were hauling out our kayaks, one of the tourist launches came into view. Playing in its bow wave we sighted black fins! "Dolphins!" the cry went out. With my tired muscles suddenly rejuvenated, I got my kayak back in the water and soon up on the plane. I raced towards the dolphins, with my friends following close behind. Luckily the launch had stopped and was doing a small circuit to give the tourists value for money as well as boosting Kodak's profits. Soon it moved away, and the 20 or so bottlenose dolphins decided that we looked far more interesting than the usual, boring old tourist launch. To our delight they stayed and played with us. For the next 20 minutes they provided us with excitement beyond belief.

'I soon realised that the faster I paddled the more the dolphins responded. Often two at a time would appear either side of my kayak, and suddenly I would find myself rising up on their pressure wave and surfing along without paddling at all. At times my kayak, which has a tendency to nose-dive, would be rocketing along with the bow just under the water. It took all my skills to stay under control.

'It is interesting to note that there is a role reversal here, as normally when dolphins ride the bow wave of boats they are the ones getting the free ride. In this case . . . it was *me*!

'As all this commotion and excitement was going on, the sea all around was stirred like a cauldron as dolphins clicked and squeaked, humans yelled and screamed in sheer ecstasy. Again and again we circled around, until we had to stop the game because of severe exhaustion and hunger.

'My next trip was even more exciting. This time I had my other kayak, which is bigger—6 metres (a sea kayak; the length gives it much more control)—but the dolphins had to work harder to get me up and surfing! It was quite choppy, and I was heading into the waves as the mammals were pushing me along, sometimes right through the waves. The rides would last from 10 to 20 seconds, then the dolphins would rise up and quickly turn away. Each of us would have a "spell", and then away we would go again.

'On my third amazing encounter with the dolphins of Milford Sound, I spent two hours with about 30 of them and I rode with them for around 8 kilometres out towards the open sea. At times I think I was going faster—10 knots—than ever before. There seemed to be more dolphins swimming beneath me—up to six! They were also very vocal this time with their squeaking, and I saw one defecate and another blow those huge air bubbles. Sometimes one would swim upside down beneath my kayak. There were quite a few babies around, and I was giving them a ride so the dolphins weren't doing all the work.

'The sensation of being carried along by the dolphins is a bit like paddling down white-water rapids on a river. Amazingly, the animals seem to know the point when I am likely to capsize and they ease off then. It is hard to believe that I am never scared in the least. Obviously they could tip me over easily, and there is a great deal of trust in our relationship.

'Most memorable was the moment when we were right under Mitre Peak in glassy, crystal-clear water. I had the sensation that the water wasn't there as these beautiful animals played under me.'

Part Three:
The Modern Era

'As far as our ability to act as social beings is concerned, we may be inferior to the cetaceans.'

—Dr Lyall Watson

18: Commercial Dolphin Swimming Operations

For me dolphin swimming entered a new era in 1992, when I found myself on a fast catamaran at Kaikoura: a commercial dolphin swimming operation, the first of its kind in New Zealand. This new form of ecotourism has proven so amazingly successful that clones are springing up all around our coast. As I write, 12 such operations have already received official permits from the Department of Conservation (DOC), while another 30 applications are in the pipeline.

In late February this is how I recorded my initiation. I felt like Wilbur Wright boarding a commercial aircraft!

At first light six boatloads of whale- and dolphin-lovers trundle backwards on wheels from the South Bay car park into the harbourless Kaikoura ocean. Four roar off to see the sperm whales. Two zoom down the coast to encounter dusky dolphins.

Facing inboard, I brace my legs in the seat opposite, where two young backpackers in hired wetsuits laugh and joke in German. Around me in the small cabin and cockpit aft jolt 14 backpackers from Europe: she looks Japanese, but comes from Sweden; a Canadian girl; a New Zealander in felt hat and khaki shorts, oddly clutching a shiny leather valise in his lap . . . The roar of twin diesels destroys any attempt at communication.

I have mixed feelings. The operators of *Dolphin Encounters* seem blithely confident, but 20 years of meeting wild dolphins tells me this is hopeless. Outside that remote spotted dolphin tribe in the Bahamas that I described in my last book, and a group of spinner dolphins near a forbidden military base off the Brazilian coast, there are few places on Earth where wild dolphins can be expected to hang around if people leap in on them. Certainly it is not predictable enough to establish a daily tourist venture around it. Our Project Interlock has a global network, and the files show that wild dolphin encounters may occur by chance, and in a few places people catch glimpses of them while being towed on a "mermaid line" . . .

(Please note: since I wrote this piece things have changed dramatically in New Zealand.)

I'd been flown to Kaikoura by the Department of Conservation to address a workshop set up to regulate commercial dolphin swimming ventures. It opened with a lecture by Dr Bernd Wursig, a world expert on dusky dolphins. He explained their ecology and social behaviour and suggested precautions if dolphin tourism was to be fitted into their scene without undue disruption. Of course the licensed operators knew that, unless they got it right, the dolphins would avoid their boats, so they were all ears.

To my surprise, Bernd told us these kiwi duskies were different from their much-studied South American relatives. Off Patagonia, dusky dolphins round up anchovy schools by day and feed co-operatively. To expect hunting dolphins to stop and play is not wise. But at Kaikoura, with its almost bottomless depths so close inshore, nutrient upwellings create food resources. At dusk plankton-feeding squid rise from the depths, where sperm whales hunt them all day to within dolphin range. Bernd urged that dolphin nursery groups be avoided, but otherwise it was over to the operators to establish an appropriate code of etiquette if they wanted to sustain encounters. However, DOC used the meeting to set up some strict guidelines. It seems that the Kaikoura duskies are mostly night feeders eager to be entertained by humans during the day. The dolphin swimming industry is in its third summer of growth and could outstrip the phenomenal whale-watch industry in popularity, especially among the young, adventure-seeking tourists.

The boat slows down. Is this it? Cohorts of black fins flash and vanish on a dark, choppy sea. Hunting leaps and high-energy swimming denote a feeding group. Along a tidal interface, terns dive and circle: a food-rich zone marked by scraps of seaweed and plankton litter. Schoolfish. Leave them to it.

The vessel is gunned up, and we skitter over wave crests until we are off Goose Bay—12 kilometres south of our starting point on Kaikoura Peninsula. Around us, a group of duskies is in play mood. As we move at a slow wallow, they accompany us with exuberant leaps. The boat stops. They hang around. Masks, snorkels and fins are donned. For safety, there are no weight belts.

'Make noises and swim playfully,' says the operator. 'Slip in quietly. Remember—you're here to entertain *them.*' I like that advice.

Into the stinging cold of the sea we go. If only I had my thick wetsuit, or even a hire suit, but air travel demands certain sacrifices.

A group of sleek duskies buzz me. I spiral, twist and spin—as acrobatically as possible without lead weights. The dolphins slow down and pass quietly. Eye contact.

'A circular mark at the right pectoral fin base,' I observe.

'Blue mask, orange breath tube, yellow fins,' they think.

(Realistically, dolphins would see us in tones of grey if, as suspected, they are colour-blind.)

I'm in a raft of squealing, gurgling, warbling, grunting humans, duck-diving, splashing, spinning, shouting, and puffing, with dolphin groups attendant on every individual. My training keeps me swimming back towards the boat, and magically the whole field moves with me. In the clear water of the Bahamas, such a large group of humans would spoil the human/dolphin meeting we call 'interlock'. The 'cocktail party' effect means that just as a sensitive one-to-one relationship begins to develop, a human sees a static dolphin and moves in. But here, with only a few metres' vision, there is little disruption. The dolphins are moving amid a group of humans who seldom glimpse each other. On board, the man with the leather case is feverishly wielding a brace of high-tech cameras.

Time and time again the dolphins surround me, their diving and rolling a visual delight.

Eventually the raw cold bites deep and I clamber aboard to a welcome hot shower and cup of coffee from Dennis Buurman, the skipper. The cameraman turns out to be Don Grady, author of several books on the early whaling days. Now he's doing one on whale watching at Kaikoura.

We watch the last two remnants of our human pod. They're still hard at it, close by the stern with duskies cavorting and copulating joyfully around them. Do they want the humans to mimic this? Eventually the operators have to haul them in. Time is up. A slender Canadian girl and an equally slim English boy stumble aboard, shivering and grinning. For one and a half hours they'd become sea people, and the dolphins didn't want them to leave. Neither had ever swum with a dolphin before. I guess they were feeling the same exhilaration I did when I first swam with dolphins in 1975.

Now, as *Dolphin Encounters* bounced homeward that cold, grey morning in Kaikoura, I had time to put this latest encounter in perspective. What is happening on that stretch of South Island coast is unique. Nowhere in the world is dolphin swimming approached on this scale. Obviously the duskies adore it: a bunch of high-energy young humans really stimulates their interest. If they didn't like it, they would vanish in a flash.

The operators have agreed never to push it. Their livelihood depends on getting human/dolphin etiquette right. I just hope the novelty doesn't wear off for the dolphins.

Since then, a magical process has unfolded—it's all like a dream for Jan and me. At ideal places around the New Zealand coast, DOC-licensed offshoots of the Kaikoura dolphin swimming business have developed— in three cases initiated by people who had gained experience with the industry at Kaikoura.

Following the pattern Jan and I had established of gaining the trust of local dolphins, by visiting them regularly for a year with the same small boat, but *never* intruding or harassing them in *the least way*, New Zealanders have discovered how to establish the dolphins' trust and acceptance of swimmers.

On the world scene, such situations are extremely rare—hence the immense interest of overseas tourists. At the Kaikoura seminar I reviewed the meagre possibilities abroad. In Australia there are the regular fish-fed, beach-visiting dolphins at Monkey Mia, north of Perth, but swimming is actively discouraged. A parallel situation has been created to the south at Bunbury: there you can swim with a small group in the river. At Tangalooma, near Brisbane, another Monkey Mia parallel has been created—but no swimming. Near Melbourne, at the mouth of Port Phillip Bay, visitors are towed on a mermaid rope, arm in a loop, and visited by the resident bottlenose tribe. But you must hold that rope!

Over in Key West, Florida, Roy Canning takes people to meet a local pod of bottlenose, but encounters are usually low key. Tourists are usually quite content with brief glimpses while on a towline. Ron knows never to push it.

In the Straits of Gibraltar, dolphin-watch trips take tourists to see common dolphins, but the dolphins avoid swimmers.

In Hawaii the spinner dolphins are nocturnal squid feeders and avoid attempts by tourists to crash into their rest periods, when they cruise together in quiet bays.

At the remote island of Fernando de Noronha, 300 kilometres off the Brazilian coast, a tightly regulated trickle of tourists successfully meet a resting but sociable pod of Atlantic spinners.

The most successful and long-term human/dolphin encounter situation is the remotest of all: the tribe of Atlantic spotted dolphins that live around the treasure galleon *Maravilla* in the northern Bahamas. But that rapport only developed under unique circumstances: treasure divers were working in isolation, day and night for seven years, with dolphins their only recreation and no outside interference. Nowadays two charter boat visit the Bahamas dolphins. Conditions can be utterly paradisiacal: gin-clear, tepid water over shallow white sand. But it is a long ocean journey to an exposed location subject to sudden storms.

At Kaikoura you can nip out for a dolphin swim before breakfast.

And, from the north to the south of New Zealand, you can meet five species of dolphins, each at an appropriate time and location according to seasonal movements. New Zealand is truly the dolphin swimming capital of the world.

In the Bay of Islands, two operators, at Paihia and at Russell, take people in all seasons to meet groups of bottlenose out in the vast bay and up as far as the Cavalli Islands. The most intensive time is from

September to December, as there are also whales and large numbers of common dolphins around. The latter may be met at all times, other than April to June. Brydes whales or orca may be encountered all year round. Minke, sei, *Pseudorca*, pilot whales, humpback, and southern rights may appear during spring to early summer.

Off the Coromandel coast, bottlenose, common, and occasionally Risso's dolphins are encountered, as well as orca, sei and minke whales. An operator with a glass-bottom boat runs out from Whitianga, spring to autumn, to the Mercury Islands, the Aldermen, and up as far as Great Barrier Island.

Out from Whakatane at all seasons an operator introduces swimmers to resident common dolphins around Whale Island and the adjacent coast. A guide accompanies visitors on all swims. Occasionally bottlenose are met.

In the Marlborough Sounds, from a base in Picton, an operator will take you to meet dusky dolphins in Cloudy Bay in spring and autumn; bottlenose are met all year around, but seem particularly friendly in winter; Hector's and common dolphins are also encountered. Six species of whale may be seen in the Sounds, especially in winter.

Off Kaikoura, from October to April, it is the mecca for dusky dolphins. Two operators take swimmers to meet these noisy, eager interlockers. There are also Hector's and common dolphins in summer—and friendly seals! January and February offer the most settled weather conditions. Visits to see sperm whales (best from April to August) can only be made with licensed whale-watch operators.

Porpoise Bay, in the Catlins area of Southland, is one of the best places to meet friendly Hector's dolphins. You can simply swim out from the beach and surf with them. But if you want to encounter them in slightly clearer water, or view them from above, you can travel out by a licensed dolphin swimming boat.

Meeting the 'A' Pod

Because of their regular contacts and high degree of interest, dolphin swimming operators are making some of the first long-term studies of New Zealand dolphin pod social structures and behaviour. As yet in its early stages, such a body of knowledge will form a base for the future study and protection of our dolphins.

An example is this February 1994 report from Jo Berghan, dolphin guide on board Dolphin Encounters' vessel *Tutunui*.

'The "A" pod is nomadic and has visited the Bay of Islands for around six weeks each summer for the past three years. A readily identifiable pod member is Quasi, a very deformed female. She has a large, deep cut across her topside, in front of her dorsal fin. Initially Quasi had only a bump the size of a fist behind her dorsal, but it had grown into a large hump by last summer—possibly a tumour? However, she is a very active dolphin and shows great curiosity around our vessel. She can move rapidly, if not a little strangely, but seems to be well protected by the other dolphins.

'This pod stranded on mud flats in Kaipara Harbour in August 1993. At this stage Quasi's cut was fresh, very deep, and would gape open each time she moved. It was heavily infected with sea lice. The Project Jonah rescue team contemplated euthanasia, as they were unaware of her past history and thought her deformity might be a pregnancy problem. But finding her fit and able, she was released with the pod, only to appear in the Bay of Islands in early December. Quasi's cut is now healing well: it is still rather raw looking but appears to be knitting from the bottom up.

'In "A" pod Mischief is my favourite. She is just so cheeky. She seems to recognise my signature whistle (everyone thinks I'm nuts, but dolphins have a signature whistle, so why shouldn't I have one?) She will come to me on the bow now, making lots of eye contact and bubble gulps. Sometimes she makes this strange "Whup!" sound. The first time I saw her, she came to the bow and eyeballed me. Then she started banging the hull with her head. She then rolled on her side and looked right at me. (Really intense—I've never had such long eye contact.) Then she started hooking her tail fluke under the hull, resting her head against the hull, and lying there enjoying the ride. Once again she started thumping the hull, actually raising the bow! It was no mean feat, as *Tutunui* is a big boat! Andrew, our skipper, said he thought we had hit a sandbar, and passengers literally fell over. The other dolphins began thumping too.

'Mischief then started rolling belly up. I was desperately trying to get a sex identification on her, but she would never keep still long enough to get a good look. In the end I threw up my hands in frustration and turned away. When I looked back, she was lying there upside down and stayed that way for about ten seconds. Definitely female! No sign of pregnancy or lactation.

'During January we witnessed some amazing mating frenzies. The females had bright-pink bellies, and very extended nipples and genital openings.

'Anyway, Mischief now lets me know she's there by banging the hull a few times. If "A" pod follows the previous years' patterns, no doubt they will leave in a few weeks' time. I really hope not. I'll miss Mischief!'

Operator	Base	Cost ($)	Frequency	Duration (Hours)	Seasonal Aspects	Boat Type and Size (Metres)	% Contacts in Best Months	Average Encounter Duration
Dolphin Discoveries	Russell	60	3 x day	4	all year	2 x 6.6, o/b	90	15 min.
Dolphin Encounters, Fullers Northland	Paihia	65	2 x day	3	all year	Jetcat 11	new operation	–
Mercury Bay Seafaris	Whitianga	70	on demand	3	Oct.-May	twin o/b 7.2	100	2-30 min.
Dolphins Downunder	Whakatane	70	3 x day	3	all year	twin o/b 6.0	70	5-10 min.
Dolphin Watch Marlborough	Picton	75	2 x day	3.5	all year	sterndr. 8.5	new operation	*
Dolphin Encounters	Kaikoura	75	3 x day	3	Oct.-April	8.0, 8.8	99.5	1-1.5 hr.
New Zealand Sea Adventures	Kaikoura	75	2 x day	3	Oct.-April	o/b 9.0	–	20 min.
Koramika Charters	Catlins	35-45	on demand	1-1.25	Jan-April	sterndr. 8.0	100	20-30 min.

* 'Bottlenose won't leave us in winter.'

Spectator and child rates are offered in all cases. Wetsuits and snorkel gear are supplied by all operators.

Dolphin Swimming Operators

Dolphin Discoveries: Steve Stembridge, PO Box 21, Russell, Bay of Islands. Phone (09) 403–7350.

Dolphin Encounters, Fullers Northland: PO Box 145, Paihia. Phone (09) 402–7421.

Jeroen Jongejans and Brady Doak, PO Box 404, Whangarei. Phone (09) 434–3704. (Tutukaka/Poor Knights area)

Mercury Bay Seafaris: Elizabeth and Rod Rae, 191 Cook Drive, Whitianga. Phone (07) 866–5555, or after hours (07) 866–2213.

Dolphins Downunder: Carol Seguin and Craig Posa, 92 The Strand, Whakatane, Bay of Plenty. Phone (07) 308–4636.

Dolphin Watch Marlborough: Les and Zoe Battersby, PO Box 197, Picton.

Dolphin Encounter Kaikoura: Dennis Buurman, 58 West End, Kaikoura. Phone (03) 319–6777.

New Zealand Sea Adventures: Brent McFadden, PO Box 85 Kaikoura. Phone (03) 319–6622.

Kaikoura Whale Watch Tours: Whaleway Station, PO Box 89, Kaikoura. Phone (03) 319–6767.

Akaroa Harbour Cruises: Durelle and Ron Bingham, Beach Road, Akaroa. Phone (03) 304–7640. (See Hector's dolphins, November–April.)

Koramika Charters: Ivan McIntosh, 84 Ethel Street, Invercargill. Phone (03) 216–5931.

N.B. Hector's dolphins have become more trusting towards swimmers from a familiar boat than myriad swimmers from the beach, some of whom may grab at them.

Conclusion: Project Interlock International

Feedback from our Project Interlock newsletters has broadened the scope of our interests even further: Jan and I receive accounts of playful interaction from surfers, yachting people, fishermen, long-distance swimmers and beach strollers. Our files have extended to include anecdotes in which dolphins have assisted mariners in trouble, warning them from danger or guiding them to safety, and others in which dolphins rescued swimmers. We ourselves were involved with a stranded dolphin and helped rescue a minke whale. We collect accounts of strandings in which human rescuers have responded in a communicative and resourceful manner. We receive accounts of dolphins caring for their dead and most unusual interactions between dolphins and dogs.

I have made a special worldwide study of what we refer to as the 'Opo phenomenon': episodes in which lone dolphins have spent some period of time in free association with humans. For the want of a label, I coined the acronym DINT—'dolphin-initiated interlock'.

We now have so many solitary dolphin stories from New Zealand that I am preparing a companion volume to this, devoted to the study.

We collect stories of fishing fatalities involving dolphins and yacht collisions with whales. Not wanting to limit the scope of our interests, to draw a chalk line around ourselves, we collect and file episodes involving ESP and dolphins, and accounts of vivid cetacean dreams, as well as exploring various cultural traditions involving dolphins and whales, especially those of Polynesia, Melanesia and Australian Aboriginals.

Friendly Whales

It was not long before we had to open files to receive accounts of divers and seafarers meeting with friendly, communicative whales. We humans have set up these categories as semantic traps for ourselves: broadly speaking, dolphins are just small whales, and whales huge dolphins.

The term cetacean is all-embracing, and we now orient our study towards the cetaceans, although the term is not yet generally understood.

My books *Dolphin Dolphin* (1981) and *Encounters with Whales & Dolphins* (1988) have presented chapters dealing with most of these files, but they have since expanded with a rich collection of material we are eager to share with others in future publications.

We have become aware that whale populations are becoming re-established globally with the gradual cessation of commercial whaling operations. We published a world map showing cetacean hot-spots, places where human contact with them is especially easy. Even as it went to press, new locations were coming to our notice, and we believe this process will develop dramatically once all whale killing ceases, and the new whale-watching industry takes its place.

We have extended our Project Interlock newsletter to Europe, Japan, Australia and America. My books have been published in several countries, and our files have completely taken over the barn, forcing us to build a small house!

The Future of Dolphins

At Freeport in the Bahamas dolphins are held in pens to be released to the sea for scuba-diving tourists, receiving fish rewards for interacting with them. Then, having been conditioned, the dolphins return to their pens.

At Cancun resort in Central America a 'multi-sensorial' centre claims to enable 'wired' tourists to interact mentally and visually by telepresence with captive dolphins at a nearby research facility.

At Eilat in the Red Sea dolphins captured in Japan and the Black Sea are held in a netted-off bay for tourists. Pregnant women are invited to come there to give birth in water with the hype that they will be 'aided by dolphins as midwives'. This does not actually happen.

At Napier in New Zealand common dolphins, the only ones of this species to be confined, are held in a concrete pool for the entertainment of tourists. There is a bell above the water they can ring. It is only silent when they perform for their food. Canadian tourist Cathy Kinsman, who visited all our wild dolphin swimming locations, wrote: 'I hope all the people of New Zealand will hear and answer that bell. It tolls for the end of dolphin captivity.'

Although the Peruvian government has outlawed dolphin killing and banned the sale of their meat, the annual kill at just three seaports is estimated at 6000 animals.* Hardest hit are duskies, common and bottlenose dolphins, and Burmeister's porpoise, all slain for consumption—often with harpoons. This is a region where fisheries have been severely depleted, where poverty is rife, and where rich people regard dried cetacean meat highly, often ignorant of its origin.

* Issue 10, *Sonar* magazine, January 1994—high-quality journal of the Whale and Dolphin Conservation Society, Alexander House, James Street West, Bath, BA1 2BT, United Kingdom.

In Argentina large numbers of duskies are dying in fishing operations, which are expanding rapidly.

In Chile the population of unusually human-friendly Commerson's dolphins, which closely resemble our Hector's dolphins, is being seriously depleted by crab fishermen, who harpoon them for bait.

And on all too many coasts of the world, including New Zealand, dolphin carcasses wash ashore whenever the wind is from the sea. Some have abrasions around beak and flippers, with undigested food in their stomachs, indicating that they have been drowned by nets and disentangled by fishermen. Still others wash up, having died from oceanic AIDS: viral infections that their immune systems can no longer resist, depressed by the toxic effluent of our civilisation.

In this grim light I wish to offer the New Zealand experience in befriending dolphins to the world at large, in the hope that it may have a major influence in conserving these precious joy-givers. No matter how poor a people may be, a sustainable future could be developed by protecting these lustrous creatures and introducing them to a clamouring public along with a healthy lesson in marine ecology. As any ecologist will confirm, there can be absolutely no future for any fishery based on predatory animals such as dolphins. But, if we are careful to observe the appropriate etiquette and protect the ocean from our poisons, we can meet dolphins and whales on their terms for the rest of time.

The alternative is beyond imagining: a planet of poison seas where no dolphins dance.

Epilogue: On Play

Because of his work as a therapist, lofty Montana man Fred Donaldson, Ph.D., was in a position to learn play from children. These experiences led him to explore play with wolves, grizzly bears and dolphins—even butterflies. When Fred met the Monkey Mia beach-visiting dolphins of Western Australia, he gave no fish.

His book *Playing By Heart** is a distillation of his experience. Reading it should be invaluable for anybody who has played with dolphins or shares this dream. Here I have attempted to provide an insight into his ideas, in the hope that my readers will be impelled to track down their own copy.

Stripped of the vivid supporting anecdotes with which Fred Donaldson illustrates his concepts, these statements have a koan-like quality: something to digest and ponder a little at a time, perhaps reflecting on the experiences dolphin swimmers have related in this book—or your own with children and other benign creatures. As Ashley Montagu wrote: 'We were never intended to grow "up" into the kinds of adults most of us became.'**

And now, what Fred said:

'How can we discover original play? We must first give up our efforts to find what we are looking for . . . Original play is not a mere vacation from life; it *is* life: You feel loved, respected and eager to explore . . . The skills required of you in play—curiosity, trust, resilience, awareness—are those of a healthy child.

'One does not learn to play by reading books or watching children, but by playing . . . If you want to learn to play go to children and play with all your heart . . . Observing isn't sufficient. You must feel play. Infants are already experts. Get down. Let go. Pay attention. Be in touch. You'll learn more than you can imagine.

'Play encodes a way of being on which the world has repeatedly turned its back, and in so doing, lost the key to the cipher . . . To rediscover the code we have to be immersed in play . . . only then can we

---

* *Playing By Heart*, O. Fred Donaldson, Health Communications Inc., 1993, 3201 SW 15th Street, Deerfield Beach, Florida 33442–8190, USA.
** *Touching*, Ashley Montagu, Harper & Row, New York.

release the child who wants to come out and play with the world in a truly open way.

'Our very notion of play is distorted, based as it is, on the illusion of contest.

'We often consider play to be childish, self-indulgent, self-centred, frivolous and even mischievous "kid stuff".

'As children we asked adults if we could go out and play. Now we're grown up and we're still asking if we can go out and play.

'Play informs, nourishes and heals . . . To play with the world is to be seized by it. It is a time of not-knowing-asking questions with no answers . . . Play is an invitation to unlearn, to be a beginner in the con- tinuous process of the unfolding of new activity.

'The first essential of play is to realise the "ah" of life.

'Play issues from the preconscious intuitions of one's whole being . . .

'Play is an act of trust in life. Ignore play and you break your heart. To play is to interact with the world as one, rather than as "won".

'Play can be shared but not taught.

'There are no experts in play. No ranks, prizes, champions. The trust of play is an invitation to a mystery—and the gate opens, again and again. The trust of play is a natural wisdom. It is like a seventh sense.

'Play develops a tolerance for ambiguity in which we must expect nothing, yet be ready for anything. This requires an open, flexible mind with no fixed ideas, no rigid plans, no expectations; much patience to allow it to develop without trying to make things happen as we would like them to.'

Playmates

'You do not own or possess your playmates. Like butterflies and dolphins, summer winds and mountain streams, they don't stand still for holding on to.

'A playmate has nothing to teach, rather a presence to share. A playmate says "I trust". Period. There are no conditions, no obligations.

'For the playmate it is not the rules, or the game that is important, but the playmates themselves.

'Playmates extend their identification of self until it includes the universe, thereby experiencing a sense of meaning beyond questions and articulation.'

The Play-Look

'The play-look is an invitation, a gift. It does not seek to extract information, to "take" from the one looked at.

'Through it an amazing depth of trust is transmitted so quickly.

'The play-look can be learnt but not taught.
'Don't try to do it. Forget it. It will come of itself as you begin to play.
'Once you've shared it, you will know what it is.
'There is no hesitation in the play-look. As it connects it is free of fear.
'Often eye contact is the initial touch between playmates.'

Play/Touch

'Much of my time with wolves is spent quietly. Sybil, Nero or Hambone will walk by and rest their heads on my shoulder or stand in front of me for some touch. I spent much of my contact time with Holly, Puck, Holey Fin and Nick: the dolphins at Monkey Mia, simply touching gently. The same is true with children. They come by and rest on top of me for a while and then dart off. Sometimes they go to sleep on me.
'Play/touch can be very rambunctious and rolypoly with fast, large and energetic movements.
'Touch is reciprocal—both parties benefit.
'If touch is rushed it becomes an assault on our integrity.
'Initially play/touch is tenuous, exploratory and gentle; advances are made with eyes and fingertips. A kind of a dance.
'The head is the last place that I touch. I've witnessed dolphins and wolves who bite and hold a person's hand for making this transgression.'

Bertrand Russell: 'Our whole conception of what exists outside us is based on a sense of touch.'

Ashley Montagu: 'Touch is the parent of all our other senses.'

Albert Schweitzer: 'Until he extends his circle of compassion to all living things, man will not himself find peace.'